"Joe Stallings understands that worshi[and that Scripture and Eucharist are th[made this the emphasis of his ministry for years. His heart burns for a revival in the church through a return to the centrality of Word and Table. Here are the means for making disciples who will then go into the world in Jesus' name as salt, light, and leaven. This book is a textbook and a guidebook for renewal."

> —STEVE HARPER, Retired Professor of Spiritual Formation and Wesley Studies, Asbury Theological Seminary

"Here is a book that takes us to the very heart of Wesleyan renewal. If persons enter into a new life in Christ through the power of the Holy Spirit, Joe Stallings argues, then constant word and constant sacrament are as essential for us today as they were for Wesley's movement. He is both a prophet calling the church to reclaim its essential nature and a herald of good news that if we do, the Spirit will renew us in the love revealed in Jesus Christ, making us vibrant communities of faith and faithful participants in God's mission. May we heed his exhortation and receive the promises of God!"

> —HENRY H. KNIGHT III, Professor of Wesleyan Studies and Evangelism, Saint Paul School of Theology, Leawood, Kansas

"Pastor Joe Stallings makes a compelling case that renewal and revival in the Wesleyan tradition requires consistent worship that is deeply sacramental and faithfully balanced around word and table: faithful preaching and teaching, and faithful and continuous administration of the Lord's Supper."

> —CLIFF WALL, Pastor, Clarksbury United Methodist Church, Harmony, North Carolina

"As Methodism was raised by God to 'spread Scriptural holiness (holiness in heart and life) throughout the land' (John Wesley), Joe Stallings urges his readers to return to the 'simple focus' of making disciples and transforming the world, empowered by the practice of the Wesleyan means of grace with constant Word and Sacrament at its very center. This book is both practical and prophetic."

> —LORNA KHOO, Methodist Minister, Singapore; pioneering Director of the Charles Wesley Heritage Centre in Bristol (UK); author of *Wesleyan Eucharistic Spirituality*

"In an age when sacramental practice had gone cold in the Church of England, the Lord's Table was at the very center of the revival led by the Wesley brothers. We who seek revival today would do well to heed the theological and pastoral wisdom of Joe Stallings and re-center the Eucharist in the life of the church today."

> —DREW MCINTYRE, Pastor, Grace United Methodist Church, Greensboro, North Carolina

"This book is filled with insights into one thoughtful pastor's spiritual journey and insights into the theological culture of Wesleyan and Methodist life. Implicitly, Dr. Stallings shows that Scripture, tradition, experience, and reason provide the resources to understand why the Bible, the Lord's Table, and the path of Christian discipleship are inseparable means of God's grace. He emphasizes that if worship is constantly centered on Word and Sacrament, grace abounds in disciplined Christian living. His book celebrates the constant power of God's grace in the past, with the present, and for the future of the church, with great hope."

—WILLIAM B. LAWRENCE, Professor Emeritus of American Church History, Perkins School of Theology, Southern Methodist University; Research Fellow, Duke Center for Studies in the Wesleyan Tradition

"In *Unleashing the Work of God*, Dr. Stallings has done for the Wesleyan tradition what Jesus did for his disciples by challenging them to practice incarnational Christianity through their constant sharing of the sacrament of the Lord's Supper. While most faith traditions value the life-changing impact of the Word of God proclaimed, only some have practiced the formative value of regular, weekly Communion. Sadly, many traditions have not yet experienced the disciple-nurturing power of sharing this holy meal as well as Scripture every time they assemble for worship. As our bodies cannot live without ingesting nutrients on a regular basis, so the body of Christ must share this bread and cup often to nourish its discipleship. Through this challenging book, may the people called Methodist—and all of Christ's people—experience renewal at the banquet table of the Lord."

—TOM STEPHENSON, Pastor, First Christian Church (Disciples of Christ), Wilmington, Ohio

"Jesus Christ speaks as the Word of God and works in Sacrament. Therefore, the Church's clergy should be uncompromisingly committed to Word and Sacrament ministry. Joe Stallings powerfully makes this case by relying on Scripture, the Church Fathers, the Reformers, the Wesleys, and many contemporaries. As a pastor, he refers to his own ministerial experience, and he writes clearly for all. For decades, The United Methodist Church and other churches have feverishly tried every available means of renewal. Here Rev. Stallings proposes that the Church simply invite Jesus Christ into its midst. What a novel idea."

—PAUL T. STALLSWORTH, Pastor, Whiteville United Methodist Church, Whiteville, North Carolina; Editor/President of *Lifewatch*

"Dr. Joe Stallings is a United Methodist pastor committed to the recovery of Wesleyan theology and the Wesleyan way of being the church in the world. This book is an important step forward in that recovery. While many UM pastors acknowledge John Wesley's charge for the people called Methodists to constantly celebrate the Sacrament of Holy Communion, Joe has not only acknowledged it, but put it into practice in his ministry. This work is a solid and sound presentation of why a truly Wesleyan understanding of our sacramental heritage necessitates not only the Word proclaimed, but also the full recovery of the practice of Constant Communion in the worship life of the church."

—ALLAN R. BEVERE, Pastor, Ashland First United Methodist Church
and Professional Fellow in Theology, Ashland Theological Seminary,
Ashland, Ohio; author of *Who Is Jesus*

"In recent times, many have lamented the spiritual and numerical decline of the American connection of The United Methodist Church. Just as many have proposed untenable solutions to the current malaise. Many imagine that the UMC will be raised from the dead if it aligns with the prevailing values of the secular society. In *Unleashing the Work of God*, Joe Stallings properly analyzes the problem and offers a surefire solution that will lead to revitalization and a recapturing of our Wesleyan heritage. At its core, Methodism is a revival movement that is fully dependent on the constant use of Word and Sacrament. This is a must-read for anyone who desires to awaken the sleeping giant that is the American UMC."

—WILLIAM P. PAYNE, Professor of Evangelism and World Missions,
Ashland Theological Seminary, Ashland, Ohio; author of *American
Methodism: Past and Future Growth*

"Methodism has always been a Word of God movement. Many do not know, however, that it was birthed as a means of sacramental renewal. Joe Stallings aptly challenges us that a full-bodied Methodism is not possible apart from fully embracing evangelical preaching of God's Word coupled with constant Holy Communion."

—RICHARD FITZGERALD, Pastor, Salina First United Methodist Church,
Salina, Kansas

Unleashing the Work of God

Unleashing the Work of God

The Necessity of
Constant Word and Sacrament
in Methodism

W. JOSEPH STALLINGS

FOREWORDS BY
Constance M. Cherry
and Paul W. Chilcote

WIPF & STOCK · Eugene, Oregon

UNLEASHING THE WORK OF GOD
The Necessity of Constant Word and Sacrament in Methodism

Wipf & Stock
An Imprint of Wipf and Stock Publishers
199 W. 8th Ave., Suite 3
Eugene, OR 97401

PAPERBACK ISBN: 978-1-5326-8312-1
HARDCOVER ISBN: 978-1-5326-8313-8
EBOOK ISBN: 978-1-5326-8314-5

Manufactured in the U.S.A.   OCTOBER 25, 2019

To Theadus, my wife,
the greatest of gifts from God and the love of my life

"He who finds a wife finds a good thing
and obtains favor from the Lord. . . . She is far more precious than jewels."
(Prov 18:22, 31:10b)

To Cassie, our daughter,
whom we love from the greatest depths of our soul,
and who serves Christ with honor

To Muffin, Charlie, Gracie, and Rocky,
our beloved canine children,
who, as true means of divine grace,
have blessed our lives far beyond human words

To the Reverend Mr. John Wesley,
and the early sacramental Methodists,
who set the world on fire for Christ

And, ultimately to God—Father, Son,
and Holy Spirit—may you receive all the glory!

I have always believed that The United Methodist Church offers tremendous potential as a starting place for a great revival of Biblical Christian faith. Around the world, millions of people do not know Jesus Christ as Savior and Lord, and I believe that The United Methodist Church, with its great size and its honorable evangelistic tradition, can be mightily used by God for reaching these lost millions.

—REV. DR. WILLIAM FRANKLIN "BILLY" GRAHAM (1977)

We move from our life in the world, through an encounter with Christ by way of his Word and Table, to an eagerness to share his presence in a spirit of renewed joy. The incarnational presence of Christ is made known in the entire journey of worship: we are approached by his presence, instructed in his presence, fed by his presence, and we depart with his presence. Gathering, Word, Table, Sending: a journey with Jesus together. . . . the order is the gospel.

—REV. DR. CONSTANCE M. CHERRY (2010)

Contents

List of Diagrams

Foreword

I WELCOMED THE DOCTOR of Ministry students into the classroom on a cold winter's day in Ashland, Ohio in 2013. There were approximately twenty students gathered around tables in a U-shaped configuration. We would be together for an intensive week of learning and worship at Ashland Theological Seminary. It was a delightful mix of women and men, of varying ages and denominational backgrounds. In the midst of this classroom context full of pastors from a variety of perspectives and places in their ministerial journeys, there were also some things these students shared in common: a deep love for the church, a desire to be better servants of God in their settings, and an interest in historic Methodism, which was the focus of their doctoral program.

As the week progressed, I found great interest among the students in our course topic: worship in the Wesleyan tradition. But perhaps one student in particular was exceedingly eager. Joe Stallings was one of those students who came ready and hungry to learn more about worship in Methodism—past, present, and future. He thought deeply, received humbly (even prayerfully), engaged intellectually, and contributed profoundly to the class. Most of all, Joe passionately participated in such a way that it was clear that this was a topic that held the possibility to change the trajectory of his entire ministry. As you will soon discover, it has.

This book is written out of love for and experience in the local church. It is not a theological or historical treatise rooted in intellectual inquiry for its own sake. While I commend the substantial academic research Joe has done in his endeavor to ground his proposition in credible biblical, theological, historical, and cultural sources, the merits of his findings point to the local church and his hope that it find enlivened experiences of worship as a result. That is a sign of proper perspective: the point of doing right theology is for the purpose of right worship.

Throughout the class, Joe was focused upon how God was not only convincing him, but also convicting him, about the absolute necessity of worship that is committed to both Word *and* Table every time the church meets for appointed time worship (Lord's Day worship). You will read how Joe's journey toward Word and Table (never one without the other) was just that—a journey. First, largely through his reading of the Scriptures and significant authors that were pivotal in his thinking, Joe became convinced in his mind that the church in general, and Methodists in particular, had forsaken the normative, symbiotic relationship between God's Word proclaimed through the text of Holy Scripture, and God's feast celebrated through the meal of holy food.

However, Joe was formed well enough to realize that understanding what should be is never enough to drive the soul to action. True to John Wesley's teaching, intellectual agreement with a spiritual reality is not enough. Truth must move from head to heart so that the transformed Christian adopts ministerial practices out of the union of both head and heart. In time, and to some degree as a result of the class we shared, Joe was graciously given a heart that burned with the fire of Word and Table— not for his own benefit, but for the benefit of his people. In fact, at points throughout this book, you will read testimony of the incredible impact a faithful, weekly practice of Word and Table has had in Joe's parish.

Yet the burning in Joe's heart doesn't stop with his own local church. It moves beyond to the denomination that he loves: The United Methodist Church. There is no question that his zeal for Methodism is deep. He therefore offers not only the findings of his research on her behalf, but also offers an impassioned appeal for its conclusions precisely because he longs for the UMC to experience worship that is empowered by the profound presence of the risen Lord Jesus Christ as found in the feast of Scripture and the feast of bread and cup.

No one writes a serious book without a degree of vulnerability; it's risky to set forth the propositions one holds so dear for all the world to accept or reject. Yet Joe has found the courage to become vulnerable because to do otherwise would be to forsake the call of God to write what he believes.

I wish that this book could be presented in such a way as to address more explicitly all Protestant Christians, for the argument for weekly Word and Table applies to the larger Christian community. But it should at least be read as applicable to all denominations that stem from Wesley (of which there are around fifty). Nevertheless, wherever you find yourself in the Christian family, there is much in this book to speak to you. The flame that has been lit in Joe's heart can ignite a fire in all believers.

When the class in Ashland had its final benediction and our goodbyes were said, I anticipated hearing of the fruit of our time together. A number of students kept contact with me throughout the ensuing months. To see that one of these, Joe Stallings, has continued his fine work and produced a manuscript worthy to be read by anyone in pastoral ministry is no surprise. As you read it, you will immediately see that Joe has not simply written about a topic that interests him; he has written about a movement of the Holy Spirit that is not only for him, but for all within the greater Wesleyan tradition; indeed for all who seek to abide within the riches of the two-fold partnership of Word and Table as commended by the New Testament church and the church of the ages. It is well reasoned, well articulated, well intentioned, and well impassioned.

Joe's journey has taken him from being convinced to being convicted. How about you? Does your discovery of the necessity of Word and Table hold the possibility, like Joe, to change the trajectory of your entire ministry? Are you willing to make yourself vulnerable as a reader? I pray so. Because if you read with intellectual honesty and listen with spiritual openness to the Spirit's voice, you may just be a part of a movement of God that holds the potential of reviving the church that you love.

Constance M. Cherry, DMin
Professor of Worship and Pastoral Ministry
School of Theology and Ministry
Indiana Wesleyan University
Marion, IN

Foreword

WORDS SHAPE US. ACTIONS form us even more deeply. When you put the two together, significant things happen. Words and actions, in fact, form the basis of all human interaction. As in the natural world, so too in the spiritual. Should it be any surprise to us that the primary elements of Christian worship in the history of the church have been the Word preached and the Sacrament enacted? It is not too much to say that these words and these actions shape us into the children of God that Jesus revealed to be our true identity. As we gather around Word and Sacrament—the twin tables of God's grace as Thomas à Kempis described them in *The Imitation of Christ*—God sustains us with the spiritual food we need for our journey in life. We come to these two tables because we are hungry and thirsty. We gather because God has promised to meet us here. We are sent out from these means of grace to tell others where they can find the bread of life. John and Charles Wesley understood this divine economy well and rediscovered the unity of Word and Table for their own day.

The Wesleyan Revival was both "evangelical" (a rediscovery of God's Word of grace) and "eucharistic" (a rediscovery of the Sacrament of Holy Communion as a way to experience that grace). The Wesley brothers believed that evangelical experience and sacramental grace are necessary counterparts in both worship and the Christian life. John once described himself as *homo unius libri*—a man of one book. The Wesleyan Revival was, for all intents and purposes, a rediscovery of the Bible. The early Methodists had an insatiable appetite for God's Word and that Word shaped virtually everything they did. But it was the celebration of the Lord's Supper more than anything else that shaped their understanding of God's love. Nothing made this love more fully real than the sharing of an intimate meal. The Sacrament reminded them of the cross and Christ's redemptive work for all. In this meal they celebrated the presence of the living Lord in a feast of thanksgiving. Moreover, it oriented their communities in hope toward the future consummation of all things in the great heavenly banquet to come.

Joe Stallings made these same discoveries in the context of a doctoral program I administered. In this adaptation of his dissertation, you will immediately sense his passion about this topic and his conviction that the rediscovery of "Constant Word and Sacrament" has so much to offer the church today. I agree. The structure of this work follows the template laid out for all doctoral projects at Ashland Theological Seminary, but there is nothing wooden or forced in Joe's examination of these Christian practices. The scholarship is thorough and richly textured, but the *telos* toward which it all moves—the renewal of the church through Word and Sacrament—he keeps ever before you. His passion is contagious. And given the fact that he engaged in this project in the milieu of real ministry in a real world, you will find no artificial separation of theory and practice in his vision. The ideas and the practices are so intertwined that he offers no escape to a theological world in which nothing touches earth. So be prepared to learn how you can actually live out a continuous life pattern of Word and Sacrament in a world that needs to both hear and experience the good news of Christ so desperately.

Paul W. Chilcote, PhD
Professor of Historical Theology & Wesleyan Studies
Asbury Theological Seminary – Florida Dunnam Campus
Orlando, FL

Introduction

As I PUT THE finishing touches on this book, I do so full of faith and full of hope. I have supreme faith in the Christ who is my Savior and Lord, and I have boundless hope in the perseverance of the church universal, of which he is the Head. I say these things with absolute certainty, despite the reality that my particular corner of that greater church, The United Methodist Church—a branch of *ecclesia* which I and my family love and have loved, and serve and have served with all that we are for many years—is now experiencing the potentiality of an overt schism borne from decades of ongoing internal fighting and an unrelenting spiritual demise.

As I write, I do so in full view of the special General Conference (GC2019) to be held in St. Louis from February 23–26, 2019. This specially called event may very well determine, for better or for worse, the fate of our current denominational institution. I must confess to having struggled with the thought that perhaps I've waited just a bit too long to publish a work that deals with lighting a revival fire in United Methodism. After all, with things as they are right now, besides the omniscient Triune God, who knows if the UMC will even be around by the time the book comes out. But, as I was mulling over such thoughts, the Spirit spoke powerfully and clearly to me and I was reminded that he had been the inspiration for the work from the very beginning and that the Almighty just isn't one to go around wasting holy notions. He further reminded me that The United Methodist Church is just one institutional expression of a much larger pan-movement of Mr. Wesley's spiritual descendants, of whom he plans to keep around for the long haul. While United Methodism as we currently know it may soon be fleeting, true Wesleyanism, in fact, will remain at least until the eschaton. So, with all that in mind and for what it turns out to be worth, I write.

The United Methodist Church, if it surely remains, can certainly benefit from heeding the challenge presented in this text. Moreover, any and all other Methodist and/or Wesleyan-related denominations and groups, either currently existing or soon-to-be newly organized, will be able to benefit as well.[1]

Regardless of what happens in St. Louis and thereafter, Mr. Wesley's teachings are here to stay; and his spiritual progeny—in whatever way or form that we may find ourselves eventually distributed—are not really going anywhere. Perhaps, then, this project is indeed coming together in perfect *kairos* for just such a time as this in fallen *chronos*. Praise be to God!

W. Joseph Stallings
January 6–7 (Epiphany), 2019
Wilson, NC

GC2019 Postscript: The institution of The United Methodist Church is officially still here—at least, for another year. But, quadrennial GC2020 is coming. Only God knows for sure what that will bring. WJS

---

1. In fact, quite frankly, any Christian church or any Christian tradition would do well—for the sake of the greater kingdom of God—to give a serious look-see to the major thrust of this book. While I do specifically and absolutely write from the Wesleyan-Methodist vantage point—and most particularly from the position of United Methodism (after all, I am a fervent United Methodist)—this is really not about parochialism of any sort, but rather about the advancement of the gospel of Jesus Christ. All who are in Christ are really "one body and one Spirit," as the apostle Paul proclaims so well (Eph. 4:4a).

1

The Conviction of the Heart

The sign act of the new covenant is the Table of the Lord, the participation in the bread and the cup as instituted by Jesus and celebrated at least weekly by the early church. It became the culminating act of worship in response to hearing and receiving the word of God.[1]

IN MY FIRST FULL-TIME appointment, I served as the pastor of Mt. Zion United Methodist Church, near Elm City, North Carolina, from 1996 through 2001. For the first couple of years, we only celebrated the Sacrament of Holy Communion occasionally. We eventually moved to having communion on the first Sunday of each month. On those Sundays, there were several small kids in my congregation, including my own daughter, who would race up to the altar table immediately after church and devour what remained of the loaves. Our Communion stewards used fresh loaves of homemade bread that were absolutely delicious. For the kids, the small piece of bread that I gave each of them during the liturgy was not enough to satisfy their cravings. In fact, it only magnified them.

I have often remembered those Sundays with great fondness and thought about the analogy of spiritual truth that those children unwittingly illustrated. I cannot help but wonder what would happen if the general body of United Methodists, both clergy and laity, would experience today those similar continual and magnified cravings for the sacramental grace offered by God, through Constant Word and Sacrament worship?

1. Cherry, *Worship Architect*, 11.

Over the years, it had become apparent to me that many, perhaps even most, of our local United Methodist churches did not practice both Word *and* Sacrament every Sunday in their primary service(s) of worship. Therefore, many of our local congregations did not engage in one of the most important elements of Wesleyan practical divinity. John Wesley understood Word and Sacrament to be the central crux of acceptable worship and absolutely vital to people as the preeminent transformative means of grace.[2] In view of this, it seemed that its absence in the life of many Methodists may be a primary reason that contemporary Methodism is not profusely fulfilling its mission to make disciples of Jesus Christ for the transformation of the world. It is my fervent belief that by our widespread neglect of vital Word and Sacrament praxis, we have willfully chosen to be cut-off from a significant portion of God's wellspring of grace. In effect, we have allowed ourselves to become devoid of much of God's available life-giving power. I believe there are many issues and problems that currently plague our denomination that could quite reasonably be mitigated, even healed, with a general return to this historic Wesleyan spiritual practice.

I first became profoundly exposed to Wesley's idea of Constant Communion back in 1997 as I took the required-for-ordination Methodism courses at Duke Divinity School under the instruction of Gayle C. Felton and William B. Lawrence. Drs. Felton and Lawrence stressed sacramentalism in their teaching. However, having been raised in a Southern Baptist family and being a Master of Divinity graduate (1995) of Southeastern Baptist Theological Seminary, I was still growing in my understanding of, and devotion to, sacramental theology.

Over the years, as I read Wesley's works and those of contemporary Wesleyan sacramentalists such as Paul Chilcote, Steve Harper, and Hal Knight (as well as many others), I became more and more influenced by their emphatic understanding of the means of grace. Thus, as a United Methodist pastor, over the course of time, I became cognitively *convinced* (but not yet heart *convicted*) that the implementation of historic "Word and Table" worship in my local parish, including the Wesleyan notion of "Constant Communion," was the best and most Methodist way to go. However, in the past, being only convinced and not convicted, whenever I engaged church members and worship committees in discussion about the idea and

---

2. See Chilcote, "Eucharist and Formation," 185. He states, "No means of grace was as important to the Wesleys, in terms of this shaping influence, as this Holy Meal." Keep in mind that the practice of the meal also assumes the practice of the Word along with it. The meal is the culmination of the Word.

met the inevitable resistance, I did not overtly push the implementation of the practice with great rigor. The typical result was a transitional compromise from a quarterly (or less) praxis to having Holy Communion on the first Sunday of each month. This, of course, was a positive step forward, but not where I knew (cognitively) we should be in a denomination founded on Wesleyan theology.

First, it would require me moving from the point of being cognitively convinced to the point of total heart conviction before my congregants would be able to make any headway toward acceptance of the practice of Constant Communion. Second, I would need to teach them the underlying Wesleyan precepts and then lead them to the place where they knew that there could be no other way. Yet again, it would first require my own deep conviction.

God brought about that conviction of my heart in the very early stages of my Wesleyan doctoral program at Ashland Theological Seminary during the winter of 2013. It occurred during my pre-class preparation for Dr. Constance Cherry's Wesleyan Liturgical Practices class. Three books in particular had a profound impact on me: Cherry's own book, *The Worship Architect* (2010), Simon Chan's *Liturgical Theology* (2006), and John Jefferson Davis's *Worship and the Reality of God* (2010). Upon reading those books, I became so convicted by the Holy Spirit that I immediately (even before the actual class time) implemented every-Sunday Communion in the worship service of my local church. At a meeting of the Administrative Council, I announced that I would begin the practice at the very next service; I then took some time at the end of the meeting and—using John Wesley's sermon, "The Duty of Constant Communion," as a tool—taught the council members the Wesleyan theological basis for Constant Communion. Every person at the meeting said that they thoroughly welcomed the idea and were completely in agreement.

On Sunday, February 3, 2013, I and the tiny congregation of Lucama United Methodist Church (Lucama, North Carolina) formally embarked together on our new pilgrimage into the praxis of Constant Word and Sacrament. We were already planning to have the Lord's Supper on that Sunday—a "First Sunday"—but from that point on we continued to celebrate the Sacrament every week. Amazingly, years later now, there has not been any negative response. There have only been positive responses and positive spiritual growth. (In fact, many great and miraculous works of God within our congregation, including professions of faith, various expressions of charismata, divine healings of many kinds, great acts of sacrificial giving, as well as several major missional projects, etc., can be attributed directly to this ongoing praxis. It has now become a part of our local church DNA.)

But, back to 2013. God still had even more in mind. During my actual class time, through the teaching of Dr. Cherry, the Lord convicted me yet again. This time it was concerning the praxis of Word. I was made painfully aware that I had allowed my own preacher arrogance to potentially stifle the voice of God. Dr. Cherry stressed the importance of multiple public Scripture readings, in addition to that of the sermon text, in each worship service. She emphasized that this provided for the Spirit of God to speak directly to the people without any human commentary.[3] My heart was stirred by God and I was powerfully moved to again make a change in the practice of my worship ministry. For years, though I am and have for quite some time been a devout lectionary preacher, I had been very intentional in not using additional Scripture readings as they would intrude into my preaching time. Sometimes, I did not even use the recitation of the Creed or the Lord's Prayer in the service. I had been arrogant without even realizing it! For years, I had been leading worship as if my sermon was the only keystone that really mattered, and as if God *needed* my interpretation attached to his living Word! In reality, I had always known deep inside that God does not need me at all, but condescends to give me the privilege of being a co-participant with him in the ministerial process. I had, however, treated my preaching contribution as if it were so absolutely and singularly indispensable. Upon leaving Ashland Theological Seminary at the end of the class week and arriving back at my parish in North Carolina, I immediately implemented the additional lectionary Bible readings in our service of worship.

This is what is meant by *Constant Word and Sacrament*. It is our belief that if every local United Methodist church would vigorously practice the Holy Word (i.e., both the public readings of the Bible as Scripture, as well as the proclamation of a biblically-based sermon = the Word-in-text) and the Holy Sacrament (i.e., Holy Communion = the Word-at-table) together at least every Sunday in their primary service(s) of worship, then Methodists would be sacramentally brought to life again by God in a way that would dramatically change both our denomination and the world. If we were to again become devoutly tethered to this historic practice, we would become

---

3. Chilcote, "Eucharist and Formation," 68–69; also, see Davis, *Worship and the Reality*, 103.

divinely changed (God would make us into true disciples) and we would become divinely empowered as agents of change who spread scriptural holiness over the land (God would enable us to make other disciples). The basic concept of this book derives from this ultimate conviction and hope.

Just for clarity, here is our denotation of the term *Constant Word and Sacrament* as it is used in this text. For our purposes, this is a term that, though both elements are considered to be pragmatically inseparable, still requires description in two steps: *Constant Word*, and then, *Constant Sacrament*.

1. *Constant Word* consists of the praxis of continuous exposure of people to the Holy Scriptures (Word-in-text) through their preaching, teaching, and public reading.[4]

2. *Constant Sacrament* consists of the praxis of continuous exposure of people to the Sacrament of Holy Communion (Word-at-table) "so often . . . as God gives us opportunity," but at least once a week.[5]

In Wesleyan practical divinity, the continuous ("constant") exposure of people to Word and Sacrament[6] is considered to be the most efficacious

4. Noyes, "1 Timothy," 431–32; Earle, "1 Timothy," 374.

5. Wesley, "Duty of Constant Communion," 428–39; Cherry, *Worship Architect*, 11.

6. Please keep in mind that Wesley's great emphasis on the Sacrament of Holy Communion is in no way to be considered a slight of the Sacrament of Holy Christian Baptism. As to Wesley's conception of Holy Baptism, he asserts: "It is the initiatory Sacrament, which enters us into covenant with God" (Wesley, "Treatise on Baptism," 10:188). Thus, in Wesleyan pragmatics, focused on salvific discipleship development, it is a good, one-time first step—a cleansing infusion of initiatory grace. Theologically, Wesley believed that the divine grace received through Holy Baptism washed away the *guilt* of original sin through the application of the merits of Christ's atonement (Wesley, "Treatise on Baptism," 10:190; also, see Outler, *John Wesley*, 321), and thus provided for a person to have a grace-empowered start into a life of growing faith and faithfulness when guided by the Christian community. This means that Holy Baptism serves as the covenant sign (typologically parallel to Hebrew circumcision) of one's incorporation into the covenant of Christian grace and initiation into the sanctifying practices of Christ's Holy Church (Wesley, "Treatise on Baptism," 10:191; also, see *United Methodist Hymnal*, 33; cf. Outler, *John Wesley*, 322). Infant Baptism is normative (Felton, *This Gift of Water*, 10–11). It does not mean, as has frequently been misstated concerning the Wesleyan teaching on baptismal regeneration, that a person is "saved" or justified through the simple act of water Baptism. Wesley taught that we are *being* saved by the ongoing gift of divine grace through the perseverance of ongoing faith and faithfulness (Wesley, "Treatise on Baptism," 10:192). While Holy Baptism is an important first step, our salvation is a lifelong process that follows the *Ordo salutis* (see above) and is not finally complete until our physical death, or the eschaton, whichever comes first. Until then, apostasy

process by which God—via the lavishing of his nonamorphous grace—supernaturally moves co-participating people through the *Ordo salutis*, the "order or way [process] of salvation."[7] In Wesleyan theology, God is sacramentally encountering people and providing them his benefits according to their need through their exposure to Word and Sacrament. Thus, this constant exposure enables people to begin to grow, and to be sustained by God's grace in their ongoing life of Christian discipleship development.[8] God uses these primary means to functionally move people forward along the way of salvation and closer and closer to him. The usual point of greatest Word and Sacrament exposure for people comes through the primary

---

(theoretically) always remains possible. Wesley agreed with Luther that Baptism, if left alone, is merely akin to a frail reed that ultimately withers away and disappears (Wesley, "Marks of the New Birth," 1:428–30; cf. "New Birth," 2:187–201, esp. 196–201). For the grace of Holy Baptism to be completely and ultimately effectual, it must be supported by a means of grace-filled life centered heavily in Constant Word and Sacrament praxis. The key for Wesley was that Holy Baptism is supposed to occur only once in life, while Holy Communion is supposed to occur constantly throughout life. Therefore, Wesley—focused on discipleship development in the context of the ongoing salvation process—necessarily placed a much greater emphatic prevalence on Holy Communion (along with the Holy Word) in his teachings. NOTE: For the comprehensive presentation of the Methodist understanding of Holy Baptism, see Felton's great works: *This Gift of Water* (1992) and *By Water and the Spirit* (1997). Also, certainly read Wesley's full essay, "Treatise on Baptism," 10:188–201.

7. Harper, *Way to Heaven*, 23. He says: "[T]he whole shape of Wesley's theology is an 'order of salvation.' It is the story of how grace operates to overcome sin and to restore original righteousness." Also, see Borgen, *John Wesley on the Sacraments*, 44–46. He states: "Wesley's theology of the *ordo salutis* represents his systematic understanding of the way God dispenses his salvation to men. Thus, God's grace is considered as bestowed within this frame of reference, to each according to his need and situation, expressed in terms of prevenient, convincing, justifying, and sanctifying grace. The means of grace (and thus also the Sacraments) are the *ordinary* channels whereby God conveys his grace to men" (46).

8. Harper, *Way to Heaven*, 33. He says: "The way to heaven is a journey in which we respond to grace all along the way. It is a way that begins the moment of our conception and continues beyond the moment of our death." Wesley taught that as we faithfully continue on this journey, God, through his grace, is affecting a reversal in the condition of our human fallenness. God is transforming our condition of fallenness into a condition of holiness which becomes finally completed in our perfection. For further study, see Kisker, *Mainline or Methodist?*, 30–34. According to Kisker: "Wesley knew God wanted something greater of him, of us, of God's church. But, for Wesley, holiness was not something added to what we are now. It meant the restoration of what we were created to be—the restoration of the image of God" (30). The practice of Constant Word and Sacrament is the preeminent means of our grace reception in this process of our image of God restoration.

worship service of a local church (which, in most cases, is typically and normatively held every Sunday).[9]

9. Pfatteicher, *Liturgical Spirituality*, 174–75; cf. Willimon and Wilson, *Rekindling the Flame*, 111–20; Cherry, *Worship Architect*, 24. Cherry avers that worship is most Christocentric when it is practiced on Sunday—the Lord's Day—because that is the day of the resurrection of Christ, and therefore, as such, "Sunday worship was normative as early as the first generation of believers"; see also, Bradshaw, *Early Christian Worship*, 83–85.

2

The Biblical, Theological, and Historical Foundations

> Spiritual formation occurs in many ways in the congregation's life together, but in no more important way, to no larger numbers of the congregation, than on Sunday morning. Here is where the average member is confronted by the claims of the gospel. Here is where the story of Christ and his church is told, reiterated, and internalized. It is little wonder then that, every time during the church's history when questions of Christian identity were raised, reformers eventually had to become reformers of worship. Sunday morning—at the Lord's table, at the baptismal font, and at the pulpit—is the primary place where Christians have always discovered and recovered who they are and whose they are.[1]

THE PURPOSE OF THIS chapter is to examine the biblical, theological, and historical foundations for the classic Wesleyan praxis of Constant Word and Sacrament in the primary worship life of the local United Methodist congregation. This practice is deemed to be especially critical because of its potential impact on the fulfillment of the local church's mission to make disciples of Jesus Christ. After all, as Willimon and Wilson remind us, it is through Constant Word and Sacrament that "the story of Christ and his church is told, reiterated, and internalized" (i.e., it is the main locus where the faith is seeded and maintained through sustained and methodical practice) and "the primary place where Christians have always discovered and recovered who they are and whose they are" (i.e., it is the main locus

1. Willimon and Wilson, *Rekindling the Flame*, 114.

where Christians are formed, transformed—and even reinvigorated—as disciples).[2]

In this section, we intend to show that Constant Word and Sacrament can and should serve as a pragmatic paradigm for local United Methodist churches in their work as an instrument of God to make disciples of Jesus Christ for the transformation of the world. Christian worship and the transformed lives of worshippers are inherently connected. As Willimon says: "The true test of our worship is how well we respond to the self-giving of God through our giving of ourselves. . . . God asks us only to do in our ethics what we do in our worship, until our whole life is one continuous act of *eucharistia*."[3] The implication is that the power of God works mightily through our worship practices as an agent of the radical transformation of our essential being. It is through Constant Word and Sacrament praxis that our minds, hearts, and day-to-day ethical living become formed and transformed by God.

Word and Sacrament was understood by John Wesley to be the central crux of acceptable worship and absolutely vital to people as the preeminent transformative means of grace.[4] Therefore, it seems that its apparent absence in the life of many Methodists today may be the primary reason that contemporary Methodism is not profusely fulfilling its mission to make disciples of Jesus Christ. As a consequence, Methodism is also not dramatically transforming the world with "scriptural holiness."[5]

The Biblical Foundation

> And they devoted themselves to the apostles' teaching and fellowship, to the breaking of bread and the prayers. And fear came upon every soul; and many wonders and signs were done through the apostles . . . And day to day, attending the temple together and breaking bread in their homes, they partook of food with glad and generous hearts, praising God and having favor with all the people. And the Lord added to their number day by day those who were being saved. (Acts 2:42–43, 46–47)

2. Willimon and Wilson, *Rekindling the Flame*, 114.

3. Willimon, *Service of God*, 203.

4. Khoo, *Wesleyan Eucharistic Spirituality*, 100–1, 180–82; Snyder, *Radical Wesley*, 74.

5. Wesley, "Minutes of Several Conversations," 8:299.

Commensurate with history and tradition, the unified concept of Word and Sacrament is clearly found in the Scriptures as a normative worship practice of the early church. In reference to Acts 2:42, Jeremias notes that the Greek *proskartereo* (lit., to be dedicated, committed, devoted, persistent, focused; translated here corporately as "*devoted* themselves")[6] is frequently used as a reference to synagogue worship.[7] This adds much credence to the notion that, in context, verse 42 does indeed "describe the sequence of an early Christian service."[8] Moreover, Word and Sacrament is also strongly demonstrated both in the general ministry of Christ and in the particular Emmaus text of Luke 24.

While Jesus began his ministry in Galilee with a primary focus on the proclamation of the Word, he culminated his earthly ministry with his priestly work in Jerusalem at the passion event. In this way, the service of the Word (proclamation ministry) and Sacrament (priestly ministry) models the very ministry of Christ himself.[9] This concept is specifically exemplified in the post-resurrection Emmaus Road encounter, as Jesus, who was initially veiled from recognition while conversing with two disheartened followers, first opened to them the truth of the Scriptures as "concerning himself," and then made himself personally "known to them in the breaking of the bread" (Luke 24:13–35). The two Emmaus followers were changed and empowered by the *complete* encounter with the Risen Christ. This scriptural event has unmistakable eucharistic-sacramental overtones.[10]

It is very important also to note that, in 1 Corinthians 11:26, Paul uses a "proclamation" word (Greek *katangellein* = "you *proclaim* the Lord's death until he comes") to refer to the Sacrament of Holy Communion.[11] This forthright usage shows something about the apostles' understanding

---

6. See Mounce, *Mounce's Complete Expository Dictionary*, 180. Under "(Be) Devoted To," he denotes: "*proskartereo* is 'to attend to, devote oneself to' with regularity and steadfastness." Also, under "Attend To" (46), in concurrence with Jeremias, he specifically explains its meaning in the context of the corporate worship of the early NT church.

7. Jeremias, *Eucharistic Words of Jesus*, 118–19.

8. Jeremias, *Eucharistic Words of Jesus*, 119.

9. Davis, *Worship and the Reality*, 115.

10. Culpepper, "Luke," 480. While this pre-church event should not be construed in the strict liturgical sense as being Word and Sacrament worship, it is definitively eucharistic in presentation and points to its later institutional development in the church after Pentecost.

11. Mounce, *Mounce's Complete Expository Dictionary*, 539.

of the unified place and connective interplay of the Word and the Sacrament. To this, Martin comments:

> Paul's choice of the word "proclaim" is interesting; it otherwise connotes the public proclaiming of the *kerygma*, and in 1 Corinthians 2:1; 9:14; Romans 1:8; Philippians 1:17ff the apostle clearly saw no great distinction between the *kerygma* as preached in his public evangelizing mission and the same gospel as presented to believers at the Lord's Table. The eucharist for him was "sacramental" in the same way that his preaching conveyed and actualized "the word of God" in human experience; and both types of proclamation rest on a basis determined by God's free grace, and evoke the response of faith (Romans 1:5; 1 Thessalonians 2:13). Both ordinances are effectual within the encompassing field of God's prior action in "using" earthly means (words, bread, wine), and determined by the way they are "received," "believed," and "applied."[12]

Conzelmann concurs: "To the Supper belongs the 'proclamation of the Lord's death' (1 Cor 11:26), and thus the Word."[13] Put differently—commensurate with the reading, teaching, and preaching of Holy Scripture, the Sacrament of Holy Communion, by its very nature of word and sign, also effectually *preaches* the gospel of Jesus Christ.

Therefore, as shown, the two-step unity of Word and Sacrament is quite well established in the Bible. It is found in Luke's recording of the Emmaus Road event and in his basic presentation of Acts church worship, in Paul's sacramental concept of gospel proclamation, and in the overarching dual proclamation-priestly ministry of Jesus.

Though Word and Sacrament are understood to be a singular entity and are thus inseparably connected, it is still important to substantiate the efficacy of each as revealed by Scripture. Therefore, we will briefly discuss the biblical basis for the constant praxis of Word (1 Tim 4:13–16; 2 Tim 3:14–17) and for the constant praxis of Sacrament (1 Cor 10:16–17; 11:23–26).

The Place of the Word

> Till I come, attend to the public reading of scripture, to preaching, to teaching. Do not neglect the gift you have, which was given to

12. Martin, *Worship of God*, 156.
13. Conzelmann, *History of Primitive Christianity*, 76–77.

you by prophetic utterance when the council of elders laid their hands upon you. Practice these duties, devote yourself to them, so that all may see your progress. Take heed to yourself and to your teaching; hold to that, for by so doing you will save both yourself and your hearers. (1 Tim 4:13–16)

In 1 Timothy 4:13, Paul emphasizes to Timothy the importance of the "three-sided ministry" of the Word.[14] It includes its public reading (Greek *anognosis*), its preaching (Greek *paraklesis*), and its teaching (Greek *didaskalia*).[15] This is because the Scriptures are the Word of God-in-text and thus require proclamation in order "to mark out and delimit the terms of the gospel, the faith, and to forge an exclusive link between that teaching and salvation"; that is, to clearly announce "what Christians have found from the start to contain the words of life."[16] Therefore, Timothy is encouraged to stir up and "not neglect the gift" (v. 14) of scriptural proclamation that was divinely given to him (as a "grace of office") through both the charism of the Spirit and his ordination into the ministry.[17] He is to practice and perfect this three-sided ministry with great diligence and devotion (v. 15), particularly in regular services of worship.[18] Gealy describes well this ministry of the word:

> His most solemn public reading would be before the congregation assembled in regular worship . . . As preacher he would interpret the scripture he had read, as Jesus did in Luke 4:16-30. Since the synagogue was both church and school, it was natural that preaching and teaching should continue side by side in the church. The preaching would be expository and hortatory, sometimes prophetic, sometimes consoling in style, like the speeches or sermons in Acts. Teaching would be not too dissimilar. One tends to preach in a formal situation, to teach in an informal one. The difference between them would have more to do with style and setting than with content (cf. Acts 13:15; 1 Cor 14:3).[19]

The ministry of the Word, in all of its forms, is "living and active . . . and discerning" and thus inherently and intensely sacramental in nature

14. Noyes, "1 Timothy," 431–32.

15. Earle, "1 Timothy," 374.

16. Dunn, "2 Timothy," 815; cf. Rom 10:14.

17. Dunn, "2 Timothy," 814.

18. Gealy, "1 Timothy," 432–33.

19. Gealy, "1 Timothy," 432.

(Heb 4:13; 2 Pet 1:19–21). There is no passivity in the Word. God is at work in it and through it for the fulfillment of his redemptive purpose. The Lord himself gives testament:

> For as the rain and the snow come down from heaven and return not thither but water the earth, making it bring forth and sprout, giving seed to the sower and bread to the eater, so shall my word be that goes forth from my mouth; it shall not return to me empty, but it shall accomplish that which I purpose, and prosper in the thing for which I sent it. (Isa 55:10–11)

The Word is a powerfully interactive and transformative means of divine grace. For the proclaimer-reader, the Word is the divine *seed* to be cast. For the receiver-hearer, the Word is the divine *bread* to be consumed. The proclaimer is necessarily doubly blessed, for he also consumes as he casts.[20] As the Word of God interacts with people, it does so with the expectation that all of the people who read it and hear it will be changed by it.[21]

As Keck has said, "Reading [and hearing] the Bible can be dangerous because one risks exposing his life to the One the author met."[22] The Bible is a change-agent because it initiates an encounter with the God of the Bible who is the transforming God: the One who accomplishes through it that which he purposes, and prospers in that for which he sends it (Isa 55:10–11). This is the reason that the apostle also told Timothy, "All scripture is inspired by God and profitable for teaching, for reproof, for correction, and for training in righteousness, that the man of God may be complete, equipped for every good work" (2 Tim 3:16–17).

The continuous exposure of people to the Word of God proclaimed is a chief part of how God moves people toward completion, perfection, and full discipleship in Christ Jesus (Phil 1:6). As Wesley comments in his *Explanatory Notes Upon the New Testament* (1754):

> The Spirit of God not only once inspired those who wrote it, but continually inspires, supernaturally assists those that read [and hear] it with earnest prayer. Hence it is so profitable for doctrine, for instruction of the ignorant, for the reproof or conviction of them that are in error or sin: for the correction or amendment of

---

20. The proclaimer is given the extra efficacy in order to fulfill the ongoing task of preparation and delivery. Those who do the feeding need to stay exceptionally well-fed.

21. Craddock, "Hebrews," 54.

22. Keck, *Taking the Bible Seriously*, 125.

whatever is amiss, and for instructing or training up the children of God in all righteousness.[23]

The ultimate goal of scriptural interaction is always transformative-soteriological. Following Paul, Wesley thus emphasizes that the scriptural Word proclaimed is supernaturally endowed. The Scriptures are not just another set of writings. They are unique and one of a kind. Their origin is from God and their power of transformation and salvation is from God. Keck reminds us: "The Word of God may speak to anyone who reads [and hears] the Bible. This is an inescapable risk; it is also an irreducible promise."[24] Recall what Paul told Timothy: "Take heed to yourself and your teaching; hold to that, for by so doing you will save both yourself and your hearers" (1 Tim 4:16). The ultimate goal of gospel proclamation is always salvific.

This concept fits well within the purview of Wesley's systematic *Scripture* way of salvation. His soteriological understanding was commensurate with Pauline theology, and thus nonstatic and aimed always at progressive transformation. The dynamic nature of Scripture, as self-revealed (2 Tim 3:16–17; Heb 4:13), is for the ultimate purpose, not only of bringing people into justification status with God and synchronous new birth, but also of moving people down the road of sanctification and onward toward increasing Christlikeness and perfection. Therefore, by its very nature, the Word-in-text demands proclamation in all three of its forms: preaching, teaching, and public reading. This is so that exposure to its efficacy can be maximized. By the working power of the Holy Spirit, Scripture communicates ongoing divine sanctification.

The Place of the Sacrament

> The cup of blessing which we bless, is it not a participation in the blood of Christ? The bread which we break, is it not a participation in the body of Christ? Because there is one bread, we who are many are one body, for we all partake of the one bread . . . For I received from the Lord what I also delivered to you, that the Lord Jesus on the night he was betrayed took bread, and when he had given thanks, he broke it, and said, "This is my body which is for you, Do this in remembrance of me." In the same way he also took

23. Wesley, *Explanatory Notes*, 554.
24. Keck, *Taking the Bible Seriously*, 138.

> the cup, after supper, saying, "This cup is the new covenant in my
> blood. Do this, as often as you drink it, in remembrance of me."
> For as often as you eat this bread and drink the cup, you proclaim
> the Lord's death until he comes. (1 Cor 10:16–17; 11:23–26)

The other chief way that God moves people toward completion, perfection, and full discipleship is through the practice of the Sacrament. We
will focus here on two key biblical aspects of Holy Communion efficacy:
[1] the sacramental efficacy of *koinonia*, and [2] the sacramental efficacy
of *anamnesis*.

The sacramental Efficacy of *Koinonia*

In 1 Corinthians 10:16–17, writing to a certain situation of church discord,
Paul speaks of the true and exclusive oneness that exists at the Table of
Holy Communion. He stresses that the Sacrament is the point of deepest
unity of the church with God-in-Christ and with one another as the body
of Christ.[25] Therefore, for the church, participation in the Sacrament signifies "a sharing relationship" with the Savior through the one blood of Christ
and a unity with other Christians through the partaking of the one bread,
which signifies the one body of Christ.[26] The key word in this first section
of the text is the Greek *koinonia*, which means "fellowship, communion,
participation, sharing."[27] It is well translated in the RSV as "participation."
Paul is teaching that there is much more than a mere association of sorts
at the Table of Holy Communion. It is an active co-participative encounter
involving an actual transpiration of divine sacramental efficacy, resulting
in deep spiritual fellowship and oneness. This relates directly to what Jesus
said in John 6:48–51:

> I am the bread of life. Your fathers ate the manna in the wilderness,
> and they died. This is the bread which comes down from heaven,
> that a man may eat of it and not die. I am the living bread which
> came down from heaven; if anyone eats of this bread, he will live
> forever; and the bread which I shall give for the life of the world
> is my flesh.

---

25. Sampley, "1 Corinthians," 918.

26. Mare, "1 Corinthians," 251.

27. Mounce, *Mounce's Complete Expository Dictionary*, 498.

With these words and imagery, the Lord mysteriously, yet unmistakably, connects the merits of his atoning death and his everlasting life to the sacramental offerings of Holy Communion.[28] In the verses immediately following, this becomes even more explicit:

> The Jews then disputed among themselves, saying, "How can this man give us his flesh to eat?" So Jesus said to them, "Truly, truly, I say to you, unless you eat the flesh of the Son of man and drink his blood, you have no life in you; he who eats my flesh and drinks my blood has eternal life, and I will raise him up at the last day. For my flesh is food indeed, and my blood is drink indeed. He who eats my flesh and drinks my blood abides in me, and I in him. As the living Father sent me, and I live because of the Father, so he who eats me will live because of me. This is the bread which came down from heaven, not such as the fathers ate and died; he who eats this bread will live forever." (John 6:52–58)

This text, in corroboration with 1 Corinthians 10:16–17, shows that *participation* in the Sacrament involves a vital, life-giving unity between the atoning God-in-Christ and the blessed communicants. Christ presents himself in a unifying theosic encounter. All who receive Christ and his life-giving unity abide together forever with Christ and in Christ.[29] In fact, Conzelmann asserts that regular participation in the Sacrament "repeatedly creates the fellowship."[30]

This biblical understanding of ongoing eucharistic *koinonia* is strongly found in the teaching of the early apostolic church. For instance, these words are found in a eucharistic prayer recorded in the *Didache*:

> As this broken bread was scattered [in grains] upon the mountains, and being gathered together became one, so let Thy church be gathered together from the ends of the earth into Thy Kingdom; for Thine is the glory and power through Jesus Christ forever.[31]

Participation in the Sacrament creates the point of deepest unity between God-in-Christ and his church.

---

28. O'Day, "John," 605.

29. O'Day, "John," 605–8.

30. Conzelmann, *History of Primitive Christianity*, 76.

31. Schaff, *Didache*, 57–58.

THE SACRAMENTAL EFFICACY OF *ANAMNESIS*

In 1 Corinthians 11:23–26, Paul then speaks to another aspect of Holy Communion efficacy, namely the remembrance, i.e., Greek *anamnesis*. In relating the Lord's Supper to the Last Supper, the apostle permanently (v. 26, "until he comes") connects the institutive words of Christ (Luke 22:19) to the ongoing practice of the Sacrament. Yet, by using the word *anamnesis* as opposed, for instance, to the ordinary Greek "remembering" verbs *mimneskomai* or *mnemoneuo*, Paul is indicating much more than a static proclamatory recollection of a past event. He is showing that with each administration of the Holy Sacrament, the event serves as an objectively efficacious (*expectant*) "living sign" that transcends space-time and applies anew the sacramental grace of Christ's (once and for all) atonement to the participants.[32] Simply put, the flowing *telos* of the text reveals that with each visit to the Lord's Table we receive a fresh surge of God's healing and redemptive atonement grace. Therefore, the participation (*koinonia*) and the remembrance (*anamnesis*) together invoke a mysterious, intersective, and dynamic spiritual event connecting both past and present (*anamnesis*) as well as both Creator and creature (*koinonia*). The Pauline Scriptures are profoundly embedded with the truth that through our partaking of the Sacrament, we choose to actually and deeply become engaged—we truly *participate*—in the ongoing sanctifying work of God through a direct encounter with Christ.[33] Chilcote powerfully asserts the breadth and depth of this *sacramental remembrance* as presented by the apostle:

> We remember. This *anamnesis*, though, is a much larger reality than we can begin to express. It is a remembrance in which God brings Christ into the present moment. It is a true divine-human encounter. Through this remembrance, God draws us into Christ and connects us to a creative and redemptive action. Neither our imagination nor wishful thinking produces this mystery in our

---

32. See Bowmer, *Sacrament of the Lord's Supper*, 168; Dix, *Shape of the Liturgy*, 243–47; Khoo, *Wesleyan Eucharistic Spirituality*, 66, 70–71; Kodell, *Eucharist in the New Testament*, 73, 79–80; Mounce, *Mounce's Complete Expository Dictionary*, 577, 1082; White, *Sacraments in Protestant Practice*, 104.

33. See Chilcote, "Fullness of Learning," 72. He says, "To take these elements [i.e., the sacramental bread: the sacramental sign of Christ's body; and the sacramental wine or juice: the sacramental sign of Christ's blood] is to accept God's desire to nourish and sustain us, to feed us with the strength and love of Christ."

lives; it happens through the coming of the Holy Spirit in ways that often transcend our understanding.[34]

Khoo adds this thought:

> The remembrance (*anamnesis*) is seen as a dynamic participation in the past event rather than a recollection made psychologically. The Wesley brothers acknowledged that the passion [the Passion Event of Christ] was "in this mysterious rite brought back." We therefore experience "anew" the presence in the Sacrament.[35]

Further, Hickman follows with yet another impactful application:

> The word translated *remembrance* has a meaning stronger than what we ordinarily mean by the word "remember." We might better use the word "recall" in the sense of "call back"—"Do this to call me back."[36]

In consonance with the thought of Chilcote, Khoo, and Hickman, Horton follows that both "The person and work of Christ are received and enjoyed" at the Table.[37] The point is that Christ is personally present as he applies anew through the Spirit his benefits to communicants.[38] This is the fulfillment of the reality of Word-at-Table. It is the Table of Christ, who is the primordial Word (John 1:1–18), and he alone is always and forever the host of that Table (Matt 26:26–29; Luke 22:14–20; cf. Ps 23:5–6; Luke 24:30–31; 1 Cor 11:23–24).[39]

Finally, in his *Explanatory Notes*, Wesley affirms that with the broken bread the efficacy "is even now" given and that "the sacrifice once offered is still represented [re-presented]" in the Sacrament.[40] Here too is indicated a transpiration of divine sacramental efficacy.

---

34. Chilcote, "Fullness of Learning," 72.

35. Khoo, *Wesleyan Eucharistic Spirituality*, 70–71.

36. Hickman, *Worshipping With United Methodists*, 33.

37. Horton, *Better Way*, 119.

38. Cherry, *Worship Architect*, 48.

39. Also, for comparison, see the grand completion context of Revelation 19:1–9 (v. 9: at "the marriage supper of the Lamb") and the grand victory context of Revelation 19:11–16 (v. 13: the Lamb is "The Word of God").

40. Wesley, *Explanatory Notes*, 432.

The Biblical Epilogue

The early church of Acts 2:42–47 faithfully practiced Constant Word and Sacrament worship (v. 42) as the center of its "common life" and as a "normative matter of the faith."[41] Furthermore, the text testifies that the church was consequentially filled with the following overt characteristics: the great awe of God (v. 43a), the prevalent works of great signs and wonders (v. 43b), the great unity of the body with corresponding acts of compassion for one another (v. 44–46), the outpouring of divine praise (v. 47a), and the constancy of effective evangelism and discipleship (v. 47b). The Scriptures are indeed making a very plain and obvious correlation between Constant Word and Sacrament praxis and the salvific power of God efficaciously working in and through the church, of which he in Christ, is the Head (Col 1:18). The Risen and Ascended Christ—that Sacred Head once wounded unto the substitutionary death for our transgressions, yet who is now the mighty Christus Victor who reigns on high[42]—has chosen to primarily and personally, even incarnationally, work most powerfully through those chief means of which he has purposefully instituted: the Word of God and the Sacrament of God.[43]

The Theological Foundation

The followers of Jesus saw him on many occasions after his resurrection. He was truly alive! And they saw him ascend with clouds and angels into heaven. He was truly the exalted Lord of glory! And this was a great mystery, this godliness in which God was manifested in the flesh. As man he was one of them, the seed of the woman who gained the victory over the seed of the serpent for Adam's race. But he could not have done that if he had not also

---

41. Wall, "Acts," 71.

42. See Borgen, *John Wesley on the Sacraments*, 44–45. He clearly shows Wesley's understanding that the Scriptures definitively connect both the satisfaction and ransom elements of Christ's atonement, resulting in "the continuous [sacramental] fountain from which all grace and blessings flow" (45).

43. Cherry, *Worship Architect*, 48–49. She asserts: "We move from our life in the world, through an encounter with Christ by way of his Word and Table, to an eagerness to share his presence in a spirit of renewed joy. The incarnational presence of Christ is made known in the entire journey of worship: we are approached by his presence, instructed in his presence, fed by his presence, and we depart with his presence. Gathering, Word, Table, Sending: a journey with Jesus together. . . . the order is the gospel" (48–49).

been divine. So as God he was worthy of their praise and devotion. It took a while for Christians to understand all this. But the careful search of Scripture and the remembrance of the interpreting words of Jesus in the ritual opened their eyes, just as it had done for the two disciples of Emmaus. The opening of the Scriptures and the breaking of the bread! This is how the Lord designed it to be; this is how it still is in worship.[44]

It is first and foremost the power of God that capacitates people to be converts and then Christian disciples (Eph 2:8–10). Yet, God, through his giving of sufficient grace (2 Cor 8:9; 2 Cor 12:9, 13:3b–6), calls and enables people to be co-participants with him in the conversion and formative processes (2 Cor 6:1; Eph 2:19–22; Col 2:6–7; 1 Pet 2:1–5).[45] This understanding is certainly at the core of Wesleyan spirituality.[46] God is the power (i.e., "we are his workmanship, created in Christ Jesus"), but people indeed have an ongoing participative function and responsibility (i.e., "for good works . . . that we should walk in them") (Eph 2:10; cf. Phil 2:12–13). The goal of the process is perfect wholeness and completion in Christ (Phil 1:6, 9–11). In the Wesleyan understanding, this is called "going on to perfection." Harper adds, "Wesley viewed the doctrine of Christian perfection as the 'grand depositum' of Methodism."[47] In his sermon "On a Single Eye" (1790), Wesley spoke of this very thing, the intended fruit of Wesleyan spirituality, namely, whole and complete disciples of Jesus Christ: "How great a thing it is to be a Christian, to be a real, inward, scriptural Christian! Conformed in *heart and life* to the will of God!"[48]

United Methodism, in both popular thought and praxis, has significantly moved away from this Wesleyan understanding of Christian formation and is therefore not maximally fulfilling the mandate to make disciples of Jesus Christ. Under the pervasive influence of an insidious Pelagianism and a non-sacramental theology, the element of divine-human co-participation within the process of discipleship development has become largely negated. In effect, anthropocentrism has become the norm; a grave

---

44. Ross, *Recalling the Hope of Glory*, 409.

45. Watson, *Blueprint for Discipleship*, 14–22.

46. Knight, *Anticipating Heaven Below*, 6.

47. Harper, *Way to Heaven*, 81. He presents an excellent, concise treatment of this distinctive doctrine (81–91).

48. Wesley, "On a Single Eye," 4:121 (italics mine). Note the connective reference to holiness of *heart* and holiness of *life*.

disconnect between The United Methodist Church and its divine source of spiritual power has occurred. As Borgen summates:

> Modern Methodism, for all practical purposes, must be considered Pelagian, with little spiritual power and very limited intercourse with God in the lives of individuals. The Sacraments have become "empty," mere signs [symbols]; the Word has lost the high place it should have in the devotional life of the believer, and prayer has often become purely formalistic or non-existent . . . a rediscovery of Wesley's basic emphases is urgently needed . . . Wesley's emphasis upon God's work and initiative, coupled with man's responsibility, will serve as a much needed corrective to our self-sufficient, middle-class, work righteousness . . . In short, without a recovery . . . of the substance of Wesley's theology of the Sacraments and the means of grace, the future of the Methodist Church as the living body of Christ is rather doubtful.[49]

The best path of recovery for United Methodism is to reconnect with the historic and distinctive Wesleyan emphasis and practice: Constant Word and Sacrament.

The Significance of Christian Discipleship

The importance of Christian discipleship within the context of Wesleyanism cannot be overemphasized. As Harper shares, "The call of the Christian is the call to grow."[50] Willimon adds:

> For us [Methodists], the Christian faith is more than a noble philosophy of life, more than a warm, individual emotional experience. The Christian faith has to do with the making of holy people who are so formed by the love of Christ that they know the cost of discipleship and are willing to pay.[51]

Wesley understood that the Christian faith and life is not predicated on just a singular event, but rather is a continuing spiritual pilgrimage.[52] Watson makes this observation:

---

49. Borgen, *John Wesley on the Sacraments*, 281–82.

50. Harper, *Way to Heaven*, 67.

51. Willimon and Wilson, *Rekindling the Flame*, 43.

52. Knight, *Anticipating Heaven Below*, 4–6.

If we are born again when we put our faith in Jesus, for what are we born again? I think this is one of the key areas where Methodists and other Wesleyans have such an important spiritual contribution to make to the church universal. We come from a tradition that affirms the need for people to come to faith in Jesus Christ and to be born again. We also come from a faith tradition that says we are born into a new way of life. We are born again so that we can live for God. It is a sadly abridged version of the gospel that considers the new birth the extent of salvation . . . Wesley affirmed that Jesus died to save us from hell and to save us for something.[53]

Thus, one of the hallmarks of Wesley's practical theology is the dynamic tension that exists between what God does and what people do in response to the divine initiative.[54] Both are of absolute necessity; both are constituent with the scriptural presentation of salvation. God offers and gives grace; humans respond to that offer and gift.[55] This concept is what holds all of Wesleyan theology together.[56] According to Maddox, Wesley showed "an abiding concern to preserve the vital tension between two truths that he viewed as co-definitive of Christianity: without God's grace, we *cannot* be saved; while without our (grace-empowered, but uncoerced) participation, God's grace *will not* save."[57] Wesley called this necessary combination of God's proactive grace and human responsive co-participation, the *way of salvation*.[58] Please note that *way* implies *process*. The Christian life is understood to be a long journey in which pilgrims—focused upon the final goal of completion (think of the Pauline "finish line" image: 2 Tim 4:7; cf. 1 Cor 9:24–27; Phil 3:12–16; Heb 12:1–2)—must resolutely and

---

53. Watson, *Blueprint for Discipleship*, 30.

54. Matthaei, *Making Disciples*, 19–21.

55. Kinghorn, *Gospel of Grace*, 105–6.

56. Collins, *Scripture Way of Salvation*, 19–20.

57. Maddox, *Responsible Grace*, 19 (italics his).

58. Wesley, "Scripture Way of Salvation," 2:157–60; Borgen, *John Wesley on the Sacraments*, 44–46; also, for an excellent essay on Wesley's understanding of the *Ordo salutis*, see Wall, "End of Salvation." He states: "From the start, Methodism was profoundly soteriological. A deep yearning for scriptural holiness was its primary motivating force. . . . [T]he end or the goal of salvation for Wesley was always the same. While I am sure he grew in the depth of his understanding of the concept, Wesley always understood the purpose and goal of salvation to be the renewal of believers in *the image of God* in order to reverse and heal the deleterious effects of sin and the fall" (1, 3).

methodically press forward toward the certainty of Christlikeness until the end (Rom 8:28–30; Phil 2:1–13).[59]

Continual growth in Christ following justification and new birth is viewed not as an option, but as a normative expectation. Theologically, this is known as the sanctification process. Pragmatically, it is known as the discipleship process. It is, therefore, not to be an intermittent thing, but a relational "state of being" that seeks to abide (i.e., continue) and to grow (i.e., expand and deepen).[60] Wesleyanism takes seriously the deep concern of Paul as expressed to the Corinthians: "Working together with him [Christ], then, we entreat you not to accept the grace of God in vain" (2 Cor 6:1). When salvation is considered to be only justification (i.e., commonly described as a *future* act of "going to heaven") without a significant emphasis on *presently* growing sanctification and perfection,[61] it is then tantamount to a vain and potentially wasted reception of God's precious grace. Both Paul and Wesley share an abiding concern that professing Christians not quit growing in heart and life before the holiness work of God is finally

59. Chilcote, "Wesleyan Tradition," 31; cf. Knight, *Presence of God*, 134. Knight says: "Wesley considered gradual growth dependent upon a yearning for the instantaneous: those with the faith of a servant [only] sought justification and new birth; [however] those with the faith of a child [a member of the family; but even more, think Hebrew *sonship*] sought [the full measure of] Christian perfection." It is not those who cease their spiritual growth at justification who become disciples; rather, disciples are those who—*following* their justification—continuously desire and methodically seek perfection. True disciples of Jesus Christ *strive* to work out their salvation through ongoing practices of sanctification.

60. Williams, *Being Disciples*, 1–3.

61. Sadly, this thin-veneered "easy believism" (or "easy professionism") is so often the case in contemporary Western—particularly American—Christianity and makes for a largely untransformed and ineffectual church. For further on this unfortunate reality, see Collins, *Beyond Easy Believism* (1982), as well as Bates, *Salvation by Allegiance Alone* (2017). Both make very compelling cases for a living Christian faith that far exceeds a justification-only concept of static Christian religion. Of course, there is also Bonhoeffer's classic, *The Cost of Discipleship*, for an ultimate lesson contrasting "cheap grace" (a superficial affiliation with Christianity) and "costly grace" (truly following Christ). He says: "Cheap grace is the preaching of forgiveness without requiring repentance, baptism without church discipline, Communion without confession, absolution without personal confession. Cheap grace is grace without discipleship, grace without the cross, grace without Jesus Christ, living and incarnate. . . . [Contrastingly] Costly grace is the gospel that must be *sought* again and again, the gift which must be *asked* for, the door at which a man must *knock*. Such grace is *costly* because it calls us to follow, and it is grace because it calls us to follow Jesus Christ. It is costly because it costs a man his life, and it is grace because it gives a man the only true life. . . . [G]race and discipleship are inseparable" (47, 49).

made complete. In fact, the words of Maddox (above), alluding to the spurious *justification-only* conception of salvation, certainly leaves open the possibility (and also serves as a warning) that even the element of justification—without the evidence of sanctification—may itself actually be ineffectual (e.g., see Jas 1:16–27, 2:14–26).

Wesleyan Christians are called to stay the course of scriptural holiness, for we are compelled to "go on to perfection" and to thereby finish the pilgrimage.[62] Anything short of such resolution will result in regression, perhaps even eventual apostasy.[63] In his sermon, "The Scripture Way of Salvation" (1765), Wesley clarified this soteriological fullness and thus rejected superficial "pie in the sky" Christianity:

> What is salvation? The salvation which is here spoken of is not what is commonly understood by that word, the going to heaven, eternal happiness. It is not the soul's going to paradise, termed by our Lord 'Abraham's bosom.' It is not a blessing which lies on the other side [of] death, or (as we usually speak) in the other world. The very words of the text itself put this beyond all question. 'Ye *are* saved.' It is not something at a distance: it is a present thing, a blessing which, through the free mercy of God, ye are now in possession of . . . So that the salvation which is here spoken of might be extended to the entire work of God, from the first dawning of grace in the soul till it is consummated in glory.[64]

The Wesleyan understanding of salvation includes the entire procession of one's existence from their initial encounters with God's prevenient grace ("the first dawning of grace") until their eventual arrival in heaven ("consummated in glory").[65] Wesley maintained a great "practical-theological concern for the proper formation of his people."[66] This "proper formation" means more than just some sort of bare spiritual awakening or "conversion," but full, life-long discipleship development that is cultivated and nurtured within the community of faith.[67] For Wesley, this was *full*

---

62. Wesley, "Scripture Way of Salvation," 2:160.

63. Maddox, *Responsible Grace*, 153.

64. Wesley, "Scripture Way of Salvation," 2:156.

65. Wesley, "Scripture Way of Salvation," 2:156.

66. Maddox, *Responsible Grace*, 143.

67. Matthaei, *Making Disciples*, 55; Harper, *Way to Heaven*, 67–76; Willimon and Wilson, *Rekindling the Flame*, 41–42. Note that this was one of the differentiating features between the ministry of Wesley and Whitefield. Wesley set up structures for the post-conversion "care of souls," while Whitefield did not. Whitefield later lamented

salvation as taught by Christ and proclaimed in the Holy Scriptures.[68] After all, when Jesus encountered people, he did not merely say, "Accept me"; he invited people to become his disciples by saying, "Follow me, and I will make you fishers of men [people]" (Matt 4:19; Mark 1:17). Becoming a disciple (a *follower*) requires more than an assent; it requires commitment, communion, development, and service.[69] Wesley knew that those who commit themselves to such a pilgrimage with Christ will over time become his purposeful workmanship (cf. Phil 3:12–15a).[70]

Wesley understood that genuine Christian discipleship (that is, scriptural holiness) is practiced and manifested in two expressions: *holiness of heart* (i.e., inward holiness, works of piety—relational communion directly to God) and *holiness of life* (i.e., outward holiness, works of mercy—relational communion directly to other people).[71] These expressions are the fulfillment of the vertical and horizontal dimensions of the Great Commandment (Matt 22:36–40; Mark 12:28–34, and Luke 10:25–28). As Yrigoyen asserts, "This is the goal of the Christian life – complete holiness of heart and life, which is, by God's grace, loving God with all that we are and have and loving our neighbor as ourselves."[72] In the Wesleyan tradition, this is often called "faith working in love."[73] These two expressions can be described, first, as an empowering and loving *communion* with God (holiness of heart), which is exercised and practiced through doing works of piety; and second, as an empowering and loving *mission* with God (holiness of life), which is exercised and practiced through doing works of mercy.

---

this by remarking that his converts were connected to the faith as with "a rope of sand" (see Wood, *Burning Heart*, 219–20; cf. Etheridge, *Life of the Rev. Adam Clarke*, 189). Of course, Whitefield was perhaps a bit too harsh on himself, for multitudes of his converts did find their way into Wesleyan societies and were indeed preserved.

68. Knight, *Anticipating Heaven Below*, 14–23, 55–60.

69. Cf. Wesley, "Marks of the New Birth," 418–19. Sounding a lot like James, Wesley avers that faith which is only an assent "is no more than a dead faith" (418).

70. See Philippians 3:12–15a: "Not that I have already attained this or am already perfect; but I press on to make it my own, because Christ Jesus has made me his own. Brethren, I do not consider that I have [yet] made it my own, but one thing I do, forgetting what lies behind and straining forward to what lies ahead, I press on toward the goal for the prize of the upward call of God in Christ Jesus. Let those of us who are mature be thus minded." Also, see Job, *Wesleyan Spiritual Reader*, 75–76.

71. Wesley, "On a Single Eye," 4:121; Yrigoyen, *John Wesley*, 24–26; Knight, *Presence of God*, 3–4.

72. Yrigoyen, *Praising the God of Grace*, 72.

73. Matthaei, *Making Disciples*, 25.

The two expressions are interactive and feed off of one another. Communion with God is centered in worship and piety. Mission with God is centered in ministry and mercy. The living out of both of these expressions is the culmination of Wesleyan discipleship; yet, disciples are necessarily first born of deep and intimate communion with God through faithful and constant worship.

The Importance of Worship for Discipleship

It is the contention of this study that Christian disciples are primarily made and empowered by God within the context of the worshipping faith community. According to Chan, "To be the church is to be the worshipping community."[74] This is a strong ontological reality. In fact, it follows that the church "is also formed by its action of corporate worship."[75] Therefore, the essential ontology of the church (i.e., the worshipping community) and the essential mission of the church (i.e., the making of disciples of Jesus Christ) are inextricably connected. Worship involves the mission, and the mission involves worship (Rom 12:1–8, 15:15–16; 1 Cor 10:31–33; Heb 13:15–16). Chan explains:

> What marks Christians as God's people is that they have become a community that worships God in spirit and in truth. This is what the church must aim at in mission. Mission does not seek to turn sinners into saved individuals; it seeks, rather, to turn disparate individuals into a worshipping community.[76]

Such an assertion is not intended to be disparaging in any way of the evangelical-soteriological work of the church; quite the contrary. Through the church's evangelistic endeavors, people are exposed to the gospel and sinners do become awakened to its salvific truth. Yet, the point here is that deep and substantive progress along the way of salvation becomes most effectual in the lives of individuals as it is part and parcel with corporate Christian worship.[77]

74. Chan, *Liturgical Theology*, 42.

75. Chan, *Liturgical Theology*, 15.

76. Chan, *Liturgical Theology*, 45.

77. Please note that basic evangelism—sharing Jesus Christ and his good news—is a driving force at the very core of Wesleyanism. It is a feature within works of piety, for it occurs in a sacramental service of worship when the Scriptures are both read and preached—and when the Sacrament is duly administered: remember, the Table also

After all, the goal is not to create paper-thin converts that may not ultimately persevere in the faith, but rather committed and growing servants of Christ. The regular practice of Christian worship is the greatest ongoing formative element in the development of Christian disciples. Worship is "the center of gravity of the task of discipleship."[78] This is the case because worship is the greatest direct encounter of the church with the living God-in-Christ,[79] who is progressively working to remake us into his likeness and restore the marred image of God.[80] Thus, as the people of God constantly submit themselves in worship and thereby encounter continuously the real presence of Jesus, they cannot help but be changed. As Cherry posits:

> Christian worship is a *sustained* encounter with God – a journey from our place of origin (physically and spiritually), through meaningful acts of worship as a community, to transformation from having been in God's presence . . . Worship is the expression of a relationship in which the Father reveals himself and his love in Christ, and by his Holy Spirit administers grace, to which we respond in faith, gratitude, and obedience.[81]

The church becomes most formed, molded, and faithful as the body of Christ, both corporately and individually, as it continues to practice the very thing that makes it what it is: divine sacramental worship.

---

proclaims the gospel. Moreover, basic evangelism is also a feature of works of mercy, for when the gospel witness is shared in day-to-day life, either through compassionate action and example or verbal presentation, or both, it is a great act of mercy extended to the souls of those who are lost and without Christ; in the pragmatics of Wesley, evangelism is called *offering Christ*. Thus, Wesleyan sacramentalism is *very* evangelistic in every sense of the word; and Wesleyan theology is *fully* grounded in soteriology. The goal of true Wesleyan-Methodism has always been about the saving of souls (Wesley, "Large Minutes," 10:854). Wesley, in fact, made having a sincere "desire to flee from the wrath to come, to be saved from their sins" (Wesley, "General Rules," 9:70; cf. 1 Thess 1:10; also, Matt 3:7–10) as the primary requirement for entrance and participation into Methodist societies. After all, if one did not desire to be saved from sin and judgment, then why be a Methodist? In the purest Wesleyan essence, this is still true today.

78. Smith, *Desiring the Kingdom*, 213.

79. Cherry, *Worship Architect*, 16–17, 25–28.

80. Borgen, *John Wesley on the Sacraments*, 42–43; Wesley, "New Birth," 2:198.

81. Cherry, *Worship Architect*, 16–17. In the second part of this quote, Cherry cites Schaper, *In His Presence*, 15–16.

The Prominence of Word *and* Sacrament in Discipleship

Exposure to Constant Word and Sacrament is the key to the turning of pre-Christian seekers, new Christian converts, and Christian affiliates over time into full Christian disciples. It is also the means by which Christian disciples are maintained. People become disciples as they grow more in the life of God. People grow more in the life of God as they practice the means of grace, especially Word and Sacrament. This is precisely why it is so important for people to attend corporate services of Lord's Day worship and to do so consistently (Heb 10:19–25).

Being invited every Sunday to kneel at the altar rail for the Holy Sacrament, after having received the proclamation of the Holy Word, is the *Wesleyan altar call.*[82] As Methodists, coming to the altar is not something that we simply do once when we first accept Christ, and then maybe do so on rare occasions afterwards as individuals, yet only when we have some special burden on our hearts. In our tradition, we all—as a body (certainly made up of individuals, but yet a body nonetheless)—methodically repeat it together week after week (indeed, we are actually *Methodists* = methodical, repetitive in our practices, grace-receptive in our spirituality); and it always involves the ongoing call to confession, repentance, pardon, commitment, and obedience.[83] Until we are finally glorified by Christ, this never ends; for it is both the call and the means to conversion and to relentless discipleship development. This altar call is the personal invitation from God to come and engage in an intimate transactive communion with him. Christ is drawing us profoundly to himself that we may become changed to be more like him.

Holy Communion is the time that we lay ourselves bare before the Almighty and unresistingly acquiesce to his healing and transformation. It is the time that we can let go and allow God to fix those parts of his broken image in us that require repair. It is the time that we are impelled toward a deeper Christlikeness. All kinds of divine miraculous work—from grand visible miracles like justification moments and the dramatic forgiveness of sins, to experiences of sanctification and the transformation of hearts and lives, from the healing of the sick to the reception and practice of charismata to the healing of relationships, and even to more subdued miracles

---

82. See Rattenbury, *Thoughts on Holy Communion*, 7–8. He proclaims that Holy Communion is "the most evangelical service of the Christian Church" (7).

83. See, for instance, the *United Methodist Hymnal*, 12.

like the renewal of commitments and prayers being made and peace from God received—happens at the altar of the sacramental Table of the Lord. The Sacrament, following the Word, is truly the continuously intense hot spot for the work of God.[84]

WORD AND SACRAMENT: INTEGRAL TO FULL PARTICIPATION IN THE LIFE OF GOD

In order to become the disciple-making instrument that it once was, Methodism must recover, full scale, a Christ-centered sacramental spirituality.[85] Humanity lives in "a sacramental universe," that is, an existence in which all things were created by God and in which God works through all things for the ultimate fulfillment of his grand redemptive purpose.[86] Thus, according to Macquarrie, "The goal of all sacramentality and sacramental theology is to make the things of this world so transparent that in them and through them we know God's presence and activity in our very midst, and so experience his grace."[87]

The concept of sacramentalism is rooted in the (contra Gnostic) reality of the Incarnation. In the general sense, Sacraments are the connective means used by God to link together for his purpose the various dualities (outward and inward, physical and spiritual, natural and supernatural, etc.) that appear within the human perspective of existence.[88] God very purposely works through these connective means.[89] In the words of Harper, "The electrical current of God's heart must flow through some kind of 'wiring' into our hearts. In the Wesleyan tradition, this transfer has been called

---

84. Williams, *Being Christian*, 55–56. He avers: "In everything we say about Holy Communion, we are talking about the work of the Holy Spirit. . . . So it is that in Holy Communion we invoke and celebrate the action of the Holy Spirit."

85. Oden, *Classic Christianity*, 718.

86. Macquarrie, *Guide to the Sacraments*, 1–11; Hahn, *Consuming the Word*, 127; Knight, *Eight Life-Enriching Practices*, 50; Stokes, *Bible in the Wesleyan Tradition*, 77–87; Williams, *Being Christian*, 49–50. Williams makes this observation: "All places, all people, all things have about them an unexpected sacramental depth. They open on to God the Giver. . . . [Thus] Reverence for the bread and the wine of the Eucharist is the beginning of reverence for the whole world in which the giving of God's glory is pulsating beneath the surface of every moment."

87. Macquarrie, *Guide to the Sacraments*, 1.

88. Macquarrie, *Guide to the Sacraments*, 5.

89. Smith, *Desiring the Kingdom*, 148–51.

'the means of grace.'"[90] Following this same line of thought, Tyson adds, "The Wesleys believed that the Sacrament was a window through which God's grace shown into human hearts and lives."[91] With this understanding deeply embedded, there is a great need for the church to be reconciled, both theologically and pragmatically, to the usual means of grace through which God has chosen to sacramentally transform, empower, and reengender a spirit of soteriological mission in his people. The church needs to regain fully "our sacramental entrance into the risen life of Christ."[92]

Relating this specifically to Word and Sacrament, Jesus Christ, who is the primordial Word and Sacrament,[93] personally shares his good *news* (via Word proclaimed) and his good *fare* (via Sacrament administered) with his church. While God can certainly work through any means whatsoever (or through no means at all), Word and Sacrament are his preeminent choices.[94] God uses Word and Sacrament to provide for the ongoing sustenance of the church, and for its empowerment to invite and compel others to become willing recipients of grace and fellow pilgrims of the way of salvation. In the church militant, the saving grace that is given through Word and Sacrament is not merely some "spiritual couch potato" end in itself, i.e., something to be hoarded and kept, but something very good to be offered and shared with others who are spiritually needy and impoverished.[95] This is the intersection of communion with God (holiness of heart) and mission with God (holiness of life). Word and Sacrament are avenues of continuous new life to the church as well as avenues of offering new life to those not yet of the church. It is a necessity in all dimensions of the Christian life: repentance, conversion, discipleship, and mission. Thus, the lifeline of Constant Word and Sacrament, formerly severed from within much of Methodism, requires a speedy reconnection.

---

90. Harper, *Prayer & Devotional Life*, 33.

91. Tyson, *The Way of the Wesleys*, 152.

92. Schmemann, *For the Life*, 26; also, see Khoo, *Wesleyan Eucharistic Spirituality*, 62–73. She asserts: "To the Wesleys, the presence we encounter at the eucharist is that of Christ. It is the same Christ as he who walked in Palestine but yet it is a Christ seen from post-resurrection perspective" (66). The Christ of the Table is the Risen Christ.

93. Macquarrie, *Guide to the Sacraments*, 34–44.

94. Wesley, "Means of Grace," 1:382; Khoo, *Wesleyan Eucharistic Spirituality*, 100.

95. Chilcote, "Fullness of Learning," 73.

Word and Sacrament: Integral to Full
Communion and Mission with God

For the church, the practical and typical base of sacramental operations is the service of Lord's Day worship. In a sacramental understanding of worship, God calls the meeting and communes with his people by speaking, revealing, and giving.[96] In turn, God's people respond. The first response is in love and adoration to God, and then to others in a (reempowered) loving spirit of mission. Worship is a divine initiative[97] in which God is pleased to bring his people together into a holy assembly to hear his good news, to engage in his loving presence, and then to be sent back out into the world in his name. Note that the life of the church is ongoing, not just on Sundays, and is manifested in many ways, particularly in great works of ministry and mission (Matt 28:18–20).

Nevertheless, an important underlying point is that even the works of ministry and mission receive their life from God through faithful and acceptable divine worship. It is, for instance, significant that the giving of the Great Commission was immediately preceded by worship (Matt 28:16–17). Thus, the church's ministry call and ministry power emerge from the vital Lord's Day worship encounters of the church with the Triune God. This is the full meaning of the Greek *leitourgia* ("work of the people, sacred service, ministry"),[98] the word from which is derived the common worship word, *liturgy*. As Schmemann explains:

> The Eucharist is the entrance of the Church into the joy of the Lord. And to enter into that joy, so as to be a witness to it in the world, is indeed the very calling of the Church, its essential *leitourgia*, the Sacrament by which it [the Church] 'becomes what it is.'[99]

Sacred service in the sanctuary translates into sacred service in the world. In the sanctuary, we become changed into deeper Christlikeness, only to emerge from the sanctuary with that change made plainly visible to the world. In Wesleyan terms, this means that holiness of heart (communion

---

96. Macquarrie, *Guide to the Sacraments*, 6–7; cf. Chauvet, *Sacraments*, 153: "The Sacraments are acts of the church; God communicates with humankind through their mediation. This communication is traditionally called by the beautiful name of 'grace.'"

97. Cherry, *Worship Architect*, 3–17.

98. Willimon, *Service of God*, 18–19; see also, Cherry, *Worship Architect*, 39.

99. Schmemman, *Life of the World*, 28.

with God) translates into holiness of life (mission with God). Therefore, the worship gathering, always centered in Word and Sacrament, involves an actual sanctifying and renewing mediation between God and his covenant people.[100] It is an empowering encounter that becomes a springboard for ministry and mission, i.e., the church "becomes what it is."[101]

In classic Wesleyanism, the Sacrament of Holy Communion is "among the appointed means of grace" and "a gracious form of encounter with Christ."[102] Wesley, who said of the Sacrament, "This is the food of our souls,"[103] also wrote:

> All who desire to increase in the grace of God are to wait for it in partaking of the Lord's Supper . . . Ye openly exhibit the same, by these visible signs, before God, and angels, and men; ye manifest your solemn remembrance of his death, till he cometh in the clouds of heaven.[104]

Thus, Wesley and the early Methodists believed that the Sacrament of Holy Communion was both a portrayal of an historical event ("a solemn remembrance of his death") and an effective and actual conveyance of the grace of God (a confirmation of pardon and a spiritual strengthening for continued faithfulness) to the participants.[105] After claiming the Sacrament as food for the soul, Wesley elaborated further on its divinely given efficacy:

> This gives strength to perform our duty, and leads us on to perfection. If, therefore, we have any regard for the plain command of Christ, if we desire the pardon of our sins, if we wish for strength to believe, to love and obey God, then we should neglect no

---

100. Hicks, *Come to the Table*, 142.

101. Schmemman, *Life of the World*, 28; Williams, *Being Christian*, 58; also, Hickman, *Worshipping With United Methodists*, 24–25. Hickman states: "It is when it is gathered for worship that a congregation is most open to change and growth. Nothing will permeate the whole life of a congregation with the felt presence and power of God as deeply and pervasively as the coming to life of its corporate worship" (25).

102. White, *Sacraments in Protestant Practice*, 23.

103. Wesley, "Duty of Constant Communion," 3:429.

104. Wesley, "Means of Grace," 1:389.

105. Wesley, "Means of Grace," 1:389. Note also that, due to the overflowing grace empowerment given through the Lord's Supper, Wesley stressed that it should be practiced continuously until the eschaton ("till he cometh in the clouds of heaven").

opportunity of receiving the Lord's Supper; then we must never turn our backs on the feast which our Lord has prepared for us.[106]

In essence, Wesley believed the Sacrament to be an indispensable tool for making disciples. Bowmer clarifies, "There is something 'given' in the Sacrament. It is not only 'the outward sign of inward grace,' but [also] 'The grace is by the means supplied.'"[107] As such, the sign and that which is signified are inseparable and are not merely recollectional, but spiritually effectual.[108] According to Wesley, the efficacy of the Sacrament includes, at least, certain divine deposits of perfection, pardon, and strengthening given to the recipients. More specifically, according to DeSilva (following the sentiments of Thomas à Kempis), this means that when the Sacrament is

> received as spiritual nourishment, it is the health of soul and body, the cure of every spiritual malady. By it, our vices are cured, our passions restrained, temptations are lessened, grace is given in fuller measure, and virtue once established is fostered; faith is confirmed, hope is strengthened, and love kindled and deepened.[109]

In the Sacrament, God supernaturally provides objective spiritual benefits to communicants. This understanding is known as the *sacramental principle*, wherein an inward grace is transacted through outward means.[110] Wesley believed that God provides his deposits of grace to people, according to their specific need, through the Sacrament, but not from the Sacrament.[111] God (not the Sacrament itself) is the source of grace.[112] It is God's

---

106. Wesley, "Duty of Constant Communion," 3:429.

107. Bowmer, *Sacrament of the Lord's Supper*, 168. He adds: "The Lord's Supper was to Wesley a real means of grace. That is, it is not a mere act of commemoration, nor is it an ordinance to await the bestowal of faith; it bestowed grace . . . The Wesleys went so far as to regard the Lord's Supper as the chief means of grace" (168). Also, see Khoo, *Wesleyan Eucharistic Spirituality*, 180–82. In concurrence with Bowmer, she states: "Communion for the Wesleys was not only a means of grace but the *chief* means of grace" (181).

108. White, *Sacraments in Protestant Practice*, 21–22.

109. DeSilva, *Sacramental Life*, 77; cf. à Kempis, *Imitation of Christ*, 288–89. See also Chilcote, *Imitation of Christ*, 143; his is an adaptation with annotations of à Kempis's classic work via Wesley's *The Christian's Pattern*. Chilcote notes: "A large catalog of amazing benefits accompanies participation in the Sacrament" (annotation #5 on 142).

110. Chilcote, *Recapturing the Wesleys' Vision*, 72.

111. Wesley, "Means of Grace," 1:381–84; cf. Kinghorn, *Gospel of Grace*, 75, 104: "Using the means of grace, of course, does not atone for any of our sins or produce merit. Christian discipline must not be seen as an end, but as *means*" (75).

112. Oden, *Classical Pastoral Care*, 164–65; Webber, *Worship Old & New*, 246–47.

good pleasure to willfully use the Sacrament as an instituted channel of his giving. In this light, the Lord's Supper is certainly a sign, but also a *living* sign (Greek *anamnesis*) of the paschal mystery.[113] It is also an objective and concrete communion (Greek *koinonia*) with the crucified and Risen Christ (who is the priestly Host of the sacramental Table) and an active and present co-participation in the gift of his resurrection life.[114]

This divine communion and its corresponding resurrection life also spiritually unifies the communicants together as the one living body of Christ (1 Cor 10:16–17).[115] As Hahn asserts: "With Communion, we renew our bond with the eternal family, the Family Who is God, and with God's family on earth, the Church."[116] It is through participation in the Sacrament that God-in-Christ personally, deeply, and profoundly administers his self-giving to communicants in the here and now.[117] In fact, Charles Wesley even includes the element of incarnational theosis (yet without transubstantiation)[118] as part of the divine self-giving mystery in the Holy Communion encounter.[119]

The point is that, despite its inherent abstrusity and surrounding mystery, the Sacrament is an incredible divine gift that should compel all Christians to seek "a deeper awareness of the meaning of the new covenant shared in the Lord's Supper, and thus an authentic proclamation of the Lord's death [and life] until he comes in glory."[120] As Morrill states:

---

113. White, *Sacraments in Protestant Practice*, 104; Kodell, *Eucharist in the New Testament*, 79–80.

114. Hicks, *Come to the Table*, 143; Kodell, *Eucharist in the New Testament*, 73; Bradshaw, *Early Christian Worship*, 85. Bradshaw reminds us: "[In the early Church] Sunday was not just the occasion for a commemoration of a past event—the resurrection—but the celebration of a present experience—communion with the risen Christ."

115. Kodell, *Eucharist in the New Testament*, 73–74; White, *Sacraments in Protestant Practice*, 107.

116. Hahn, *Lamb's Supper*, 56; cf. Chilcote, "Fullness of Learning," 73. Here Chilcote says: "Receiving the bread not only unites us to the Lord, but also to one another in Him."

117. Oden, *Classical Pastoral Care*, 154–55; White, *Sacraments as God's Self Giving*, 52.

118. Bowmer, *Sacrament of the Lord's Supper*, 169–71; see also, Rattenbury, *Wesley's Legacy to the World*, 177–79.

119. Kimbrough, *Lyrical Theology of Charles Wesley*, 89–91; White, *Sacraments as God's Self Giving*, 59.

120. Kodell, *Eucharist in the New Testament*, 82; cf. Conzelmann, *History of Primitive Christianity*, 76.

The Eucharist is God's fundamental gift to the church—as a body and in each of its members—whereby we come to know ourselves over and over again, at times even more deeply and intimately, as sharing in the very life and mission of Christ Jesus and his Spirit.[121]

With such a divine gift so great, it is no wonder that Wesley called Holy Communion "the grand channel whereby the grace of his Spirit was conveyed to the souls of all the children of God."[122] The most authentic divine engagement in Christian worship, then, viz. "acceptable worship" (Heb 12:28–29), culminates effectually and *deeply* at the liturgical Table (cf. Ps 36:7–9).[123]

It is, however, quite important to stress that the Table should not stand alone. While receiving the Sacrament is the culmination of worship, it is the proclamation of the Word that leads to the Table.[124] Wesley, a self-professed man of "the Book of God,"[125] strongly taught that Scripture also was a powerful means of grace (2 Tim 3:14–17; cf. Isa 55:11).[126] The Scriptures carry with them their own brand of life-changing efficacy. As Bouyer says:

They are truly the shadow cast by the very Truth of God, the God of Jesus Christ, coming down to us 'the same yesterday and today,

---

121. Morrill, *Encountering Christ in the Eucharist*, 1.

122. Wesley, "Upon Our Lord's Sermon on the Mount, IV," 1:585.

123. In his *Journal* (November 13, 1763), Wesley even went so far as to say, "I found much of the power of God in preaching, but far more at the Lord's Table" (Wesley, "Journal," 3:156). This is commensurate with his "grand channel" understanding of Holy Communion. Wesley's sentiment should be understood, however, not in any way as a diminishment to the power of the Word proclaimed, but as testament to its efficacious completion in the Word enacted. Remember, the Word-in-text (Scripture read and preached) is only a cup half-full apart from the Word-at-table (Sacrament administered). Yet, when used together, the cup is full, and the power of God finds maximal sacramental release into the open hearts and lives of receptive congregants. The two tributary channels become as one grand channel of overflowing grace at the Table. In Wesleyanism, the Sacrament administered presupposes the Scriptures proclaimed. The two are inseparably one.

124. See also Senn, *Stewardship of the Mysteries*, 8. While Holy Communion is the "summit," it is the preaching of the Word that points us to it.

125. Wesley, "Preface to Standard Sermons," 1:105. Wesley says, "God himself has condescended to teach the way: For this very end he came from heaven. He hath written it down in a book. O give me that book! At any price give me the Book of God! I have it. Here is knowledge enough for me. Let me be *homo unius libri* [Latin: 'a man of one book']"; see also, Stokes, *Bible in the Wesleyan Tradition*, 19–21.

126. Wesley, "Means of Grace," 1:381; Carter, *Way of Life*, 35–42.

and forever' (Heb. 13:8) and laying hold of our mind and heart in that unique experience which is faith, faith in the Word of the living God.[127]

The Word itself becomes sacramentally effective in the lives of people. Through the Scriptures, God "is not merely obliging us to revise our whole way of looking at reality and to approach it with a new outlook that derives from his; he [actually] changes [our] reality itself; he transforms it utterly."[128] This is the proactive and innate sacramental power of God's Word (Heb 4:12)! According to Wesley, the constant exposure to Scripture, its "reading, hearing, and meditating thereon,"[129] is the means by which God inculcates the particular testimony of himself, his "true wisdom," and "the light of his countenance" into the minds and hearts of people.[130] The proclamation of the Scriptures is not merely effective in causing our cognitive change, but is soul and life pervasive in its transformational power. Exposure to Scripture carries the capacity to change the deepest dimensions of our existence. It is essential to the formation of us becoming new creations in Christ (2 Cor 5:17).

Though not formally considered as a Sacrament of the church in the Anglican tradition, Wesley certainly understood that the Word-in-text

127. Bouyer, *Word, Church and Sacraments*, 19.

128. Bouyer, *Word, Church and Sacraments*, 17–18.

129. Wesley, "Means of Grace," 1:381.

130. Wesley, "Means of Grace," 1:387–88.

(Scripture) is intensely sacramental in its very nature[131] and included it as an Instituted means of grace.[132] As Wall affirms:

> Not only does his extensive quotation of Scripture envisage a deep reverence for the Bible's sacred words, his firm confidence that those biblical words deliver the word of God without need of human mediation create a prophetic "thus saith the Lord" address. Put differently, Wesley's prolific use of Scripture turned his sermons into Sacraments, means for the body of Christ to ingest the sacred words and to experience in them afresh the Holy Spirit's active presence in our hearts.[133]

In fact, it is very possible that Wesley's strong adherence to Anglicanism was the only thing that prevented him from considering "searching the Scriptures" as a formal (third) Sacrament of the church. In confirmation of Wall's commentary, Wesley held this view of the Bible:

131. Hahn, *Consuming the Word*, 127–32; Heath, "Reading Scripture for Christian Formation," 213; also, for an excellent essay on the sacramentality of Scripture, see Cantalamessa, *Mystery of God's Word*, 10–16. He states: "Divine revelation is closed: in one sense, there are no more [additional] words of God. And here we discover another affinity between Word and Eucharist. The Eucharist is present throughout salvation-history: first in the Old Testament, as type, then in the New Testament as event [i.e., Christ Event], and finally in the Church as Sacrament. True, Christ's sacrifice was once and for all concluded on the cross; in a certain sense, therefore, there are no more sacrifices for Christ. Yet we know that there is still a sacrifice and that the unique sacrifice of the Cross is made present and operant at the Eucharistic sacrifice; the event continues in the Sacrament, and history in the liturgy. Something analogous occurs with the Word of Christ: it has ceased to exist as event but continues to exist as Sacrament" (11); he also adds: "The sacramental nature of the Word of God is shown by the way on occasion it manifestly operates beyond the comprehension of the listener, which comprehension may be limited and imperfect; it operates virtually on its own" (13). Therefore, in the mystery of sacramentality, the historical event of the chronological past becomes a renewed event of the chronological present. While the scriptural revelation remains closed and unchanging, the divine power working through Word and Sacrament remains eternally alive and life-transforming. The proclaimed Word and the administered Table are thus both sacramental—each conveying present power and grace from God through the reapplicative connection to us of the chronologically past Christ event of God. In other words, whenever we are exposed to Word and Sacrament, a revitalizing surge of the power and grace of the Christ event is yet again reapplied to us. Our souls are fed again. And each feeding is, in some sense, spiritually nutritious whether we always fully comprehend it or not. Remember the words of Cantalamessa: "it operates virtually on its own." Wesley understood this reality and utilized it. We need to do so as well.

132. Wesley, "Means of Grace," 1:381, 386–89; Harper, *Prayer & Devotional Life*, 33–34.

133. Wall, "Wesley as Biblical Interpreter," 128.

[T]he Christian rule of right and wrong is the word of God, the writings of the Old and New Testament: all which the prophets and "holy men of old" wrote "as they were moved by the Holy Ghost;" "all" that "Scripture" which was "given by inspiration of God," and which is indeed "profitable for doctrine," or teaching the whole will of God; "for reproof" of what is contrary thereto; "for correction" of error; and "for instruction (or training us up) in righteousness." This "is a lantern unto a" Christian's "feet, and a light in all his paths." This alone he receives as his rule of right or wrong, of whatever is really good or evil.[134]

Moreover, in his *Journal* (June 2, 1766), Wesley wrote these summative words: "My ground is the Bible. Yea, I am a Bible-bigot. I follow it in all things, both great and small."[135] Wesley was clearly a man of the Bible, the book of God, and an adherent to the sacramentality of Scripture. This conviction never wavered. In 1789 (near the end of his life), he wrote, "Here I am: I and my Bible . . . I am determined to be a Bible Christian, not almost, but altogether."[136] Therefore, in classic Wesleyanism, following its progenitor, the Scriptures are understood to be "the only sufficient rule for both faith and practice."[137] Wesley was an avowed sacramentalist, and yet an evangelical Bible preacher and teacher of the very highest order.[138]

WORD *AND* SACRAMENT: INTEGRAL TO FULL AND BALANCED DISCIPLESHIP DEVELOPMENT

Both Word and Sacrament are the essence and norm of true and transformative Christian worship.[139] Far too often, Christians of various traditions have emphasized either the Word or the Table to the exclusion or the

134. Wesley, "Witness of Our Own Spirit," 1:302–3.

135. Wesley, "Journal" (June 2, 1766), 3:251.

136. Wesley, "Causes of the Inefficacy," 4:93.

137. Chilcote, *John & Charles Wesley*, 198.

138. Wesley's practical *evangelical-sacramental* divinity was predicated on the presentation of a narrow orthodoxy (a very definitive doctrinal foundation) along with its correlative expression in a narrow orthopraxy (a very definitive methodological formula). His teaching and his practices were biblical and systematic; they adhered to the classic rule of faith; and they were divinely blessed and driven by the power of the Holy Spirit. For further study on Wesley's systematic orthodoxy, see Oden's great body of work on this subject, including *John Wesley's Scriptural Christianity* (1994), and the four-volume set, *John Wesley's Teachings* (2012, 2014).

139. Webber, *Worship Old & New*, 106.

diminishment of the other.[140] Wesley, however, would have nothing to do with such an imbalance. His missional spirituality was decisively evangelical *and* eucharistic.[141] As Outler comments, "In his understanding of the nature of grace and the means of grace, Word and Sacraments are dynamically integrated."[142] For the Sacrament of God to have maximum efficacy, the complimentary power of the read and proclaimed Word of God-in-text should also be unleashed (Isa 55:10–11). Likewise, for the Word to have maximum expression and impact, the Word of God-at-table should also be duly administered. Hicks explains:

> The supper is the gospel in bread and wine. As a gospel event it embodies all that the gospel is. Thus, whenever the gospel is proclaimed, the supper gives concrete, visible expression to the message of the gospel through eating and drinking.[143]

Such a dynamic relationship between essential Word and Sacrament is not surprising since the Scriptures, the doctrine, and the liturgy of the faith co-developed in a mutually informing process known as *lex orandi est lex credendi* (Latin: "the law of prayer is the law of belief"). All are so enjoined as to be incomplete without the other.[144]

Be reminded that the divine self-giver, God-in-Christ, is the primordial Word and Sacrament; thus, the Word and the Sacrament are actually two sides of the very same inseparable, divine coin. In fact, Laurance likens the practice of worship without the inclusion of both Word and Sacrament to that of trying to understand the full scriptural revelation without being availed of both the Old Testament and the New Testament.[145] Similarly, Wesley described such incomplete and impotent worship "as looking for

140. Morrill, *Encountering Christ in the Eucharist*, 67.

141. Chilcote, *Early Methodist Spirituality*, 29.

142. Outler, *John Wesley*, 334.

143. Hicks, *Come to the Table*, 139; cf. Rattenbury, *Wesley's Legacy to the World*, 174. As to the Wesleys, Rattenbury states, "there is no antithesis more false than the common one of Sacrament and gospel."

144. Laurance, *Sacrament of the Eucharist*, 120–22; Mitman, *Worship in the Shape*, 41–42; Cherry, *Worship Architect*, 137. For further study, see Jesson, "*Lex orandi, lex credenda*." We concur with Jesson's postulation that "the relationship of liturgy and theology [act] as symbiotic disciplines. Each draws from the other, and provides for the other" (1). Note further that some variations of this construct also add in the phrase, "*lex vivendi*," which means, "so we live." This essentially extends the notion to: "As we pray, so we believe, so we live." This concurs with Wesleyanism.

145. Laurance, *Sacrament of the Eucharist*, 122.

the end, without using [any or all of] the means."[146] In the Wesleyan tradition, Sunday worship becomes appropriately balanced through "a wide and healthy diet of Scripture, read in some systematic way, that goes beyond the personal idiosyncrasies of the preacher" combined with "the weekly celebration of the Lord's Supper."[147]

It is an important liturgical principle within the realm of Christian spirituality that the Liturgy of the Word and the Liturgy of the Table function in tandem. As the Living Christ is understood to be in *real presence* in a service of Christian worship, it is he that speaks to and nourishes the body through both the public reading of Scripture and its homiletic-didactic application (1 Tim 4:13).[148] It is also he that reveals and presents himself through the "broken bread and poured out wine."[149] In this sense, there is an inseparable sacramental unity between the Word and the Table.[150]

In a sacramental understanding of worship, such as that held by historic Wesleyan-Methodism, Christ personally speaks and acts in real time and space within each very specific and historically unique liturgical gathering. Laurance provides this summation:

> For it is through the Liturgy of the Word, revealing Christ alive in their contemporary world both within them and around them, that members of each liturgical assembly are able to see not a Gnostic Christ existing independent of history, but rather a Christ whose presence in the Eucharist is one with all the moments of their own lives, both "today" (hodie) and into the future: "O that today you would listen to his voice" (Ps. 95:7; cf. Heb. 3:7).[151]

It is the purpose of the proclamation of the Word to provide the gathered assembly with the objective reality of the Christ event and its specific application within this contemporary scenario of historical existence.[152]

---

146. Ruth, "Word and Table," 139.

147. Ruth, "Word and Table," 142, 136–37.

148. Chappell, *Christ-Centered Worship*, 220–23; Webber, *Ancient-Future Worship*, 113, 133–34.

149. Webber, *Ancient-Future Worship*, 134.

150. Laurance, *Sacrament of the Eucharist*, 125.

151. Laurance, *Sacrament of the Eucharist*, 126.

152. Laurance, *Sacrament of the Eucharist*, 138; also, Senn, *Stewardship of the Mysteries*, 8. Senn states: "Preaching in the liturgy of the Word cannot refrain from pointing to meanings expressed in the liturgy of the eucharistic meal. For this communion meal in the presence of the Lord is the summit of the church's life and the source of the church's mission in and to the world."

The proclamation appropriately sets the stage for the actual and mysterious formative encounter of the people with the Risen Christ, who is the gracious and self-giving priestly Host at the Communion Table.[153]

Thus, in the sanctuary of God, the revelation of the Christ event is read and explained from the pulpit and then encountered and experienced at the altar. In Word and Sacrament worship, God works through both the human cognitive dimension and the human affective dimension. God seeks, utilizes, and transforms the whole person. Lord's Day worship is the primary meeting place between God and humanity; it is the place where God most powerfully forms and transforms the minds and hearts of people and, from there, sends them into mission.

WORD *AND* SACRAMENT: INTEGRAL TO FULL AND CONTINUAL DISCIPLESHIP DEVELOPMENT

The people of God are invited to continuously feast upon the spiritual food of the Word and Table which signifies the continuous and eternally communal nature of the Kingdom of God. Word-Sacrament is both the discipling "food for the journey"[154] and the eschatological "antepast of Heaven."[155] Word and Sacrament are the "two [feeding] tables of the Word of God" that are divinely life-giving[156] to the church of Jesus Christ until the end of time (1 Cor 11:26). There is great and abiding spiritual power conveyed to the church through the constant exhortation of the Word "in season and out of season" (2 Tim 4:1–5; i.e., every time the Scriptures are read and proclaimed) and through the constant mysterious encounter with the Risen Christ at his Table of grace (1 Cor 10:16–17 [*koinonia* mystery]; 1 Cor 11:24–25 [*anamnesis* mystery]).[157]

The Word-in-text (Rev 1) strongly proclaims that it is this supernatural and inscrutable God-in-Christ ("one like a son of man," v. 13), who lives amidst his church ("the seven golden lampstands," v. 12), and who continuously offers and provides his empowering and perfecting grace to all who will receive (Rev 1:12–20; cf. Rev 3:18–22). Christ announces, "Behold,

---

153. Hicks, *Come to the Table*, 141; Marshall, *Last Supper & Lord's Supper*, 151–52; Khoo, *Wesleyan Eucharistic Spirituality*, 62–73.

154. Harper, *Devotional Life in the Wesleyan Tradition*, 36.

155. Wainwright, *Eucharist and Eschatology*, 70–74.

156. Hahn, *Consuming the Word*, 131–32; cf. à Kempis, *Imitation of Christ*, 309–10.

157. Yrigoyen, *Praising the God of Grace*, 68–70.

I stand at the door and knock; if anyone hears my voice and opens the door, I will come in to him and eat with him, and he with me" (Rev 3:20). Though the corporate ecclesial ontology is ultimately "from above,"[158] there is no distant separation between God and his church on earth. Christ is in permanent mysterious real presence both with and within his church, even "to the close of the age" (Matt 28:20; Acts 18:10). This is exemplified through the mystery of Word and Sacrament as God continuously connects spiritually with his church through the means of a physical book and the physical elements of bread and drink. In keeping with his incarnational (and non-Gnostic) character, the God of the universe chooses to spiritually and personally reveal and relate himself in and through certain ordinary means of the physical realm.[159]

The church has great ontic substance because of this very presence of the Godhead who is its Creator, Redeemer, and continual personal Sustainer and source of empowerment. Therefore, when the church becomes a gathered worshipping community actively engaged in Word and Sacrament, it becomes much more than a gathering of people practicing a set of religious rites in a church sanctuary. The church becomes a mighty spiritual body of believers ("one body and one Spirit . . . one hope . . . one Lord, one faith, one baptism") who are united as one by God "who is above all and through all and in all" (Eph 4:4–6), and whose unified worship immediately and in actuality connects heaven and earth together as one.[160]

158. Davis, *Worship and the Reality*, 65.

159. In the Eastern church, the Sacrament of Holy Communion is often known by the Greek term, *mysterion* (translated into the Latin as *Sacramentum*). This term is actually quite appropriate, for in each sacramental encounter, God mysteriously connects with us in efficacious ways that transcend mere anthropocentric notions and all human intellectual understandings. It is truly the *mysterion* because through it the infinite meets the finite, and we mortal creatures thus engage in a supernatural theosic encounter with our immortal Creator that remains far beyond our ability to fully comprehend. The Sacrament, by its very nature, places us in a position of humble acquiescence to God and his giving of grace much more than in a position of rational cognizance of God's ways and the logistics of his divine mechanics. This was certainly true of early Methodist pragmatics. As Khoo avers: "For the Wesleys, the human response to this mystery is to simply accept the gift of the presence, the fruits of the encounter, and to give grateful thanks" (Khoo, *Wesleyan Eucharistic Spirituality*, 73). This humble response fueled the fire of revival.

160. Irenaeus, "Against Heresies," 1:458; see also, Cherry, *Worship Architect*, 4–5. Following Irenaeus, Cherry adds this: "When we gather for corporate worship, our adoration is a significant continuation of that which began before the foundations of the world were laid, that which occurs in heaven contemporaneous with our worship at any given

As such, the worshipping church becomes "immersed in the new life of the Kingdom."[161] Hahn states, "heaven touches down whenever the church celebrates the Eucharist."[162] In all sacramental Christian worship, the element of divine mystery abounds.

Case in point: Even the proclamation of the *mystery of faith* in the UM liturgy of Holy Communion—"Christ has died; Christ is risen; Christ will come again"—somewhat subtly, yet very definitively, reveals that mysterious continuity of the three great eucharistic Tables of the faith in *chronos* (i.e., the *past* Table of the Last Supper; the *present* Table of Holy Communion; the *future* Table of the Marriage Feast of the Lamb), which are actually one contiguous, trans-eternal Table in the context of *kairos*.[163] Together as one, the three Tables traverse the panorama of salvation in Christ and thus point to the certainty of divine purpose and ultimate completion.[164]

Although many local congregations miss it as such, the transpiration of sacramental Christian worship is always a very dramatic event that, even in the now, transcends time with eternity and simultaneously engages the church militant and the church triumphant as one great purposeful congregation in the presence of God.[165] Most people on earth would be astounded

---

moment, and that which foreshadows the worship to come when Christ reigns. Worship is eternal."

161. Schmemann, *For the Life*, 28.

162. Hahn, *Lamb's Supper*, 6.

163. It is the everlasting Table (Last Supper<Lord's Supper>Wedding Supper) of the kingdom of God (Matt 26:29; Luke 22:15–18), and was prophesied by David in Psalm 23: "The Lord is my shepherd, I shall not want . . . *Thou preparest a table before me* in the presence of my enemies; thou anointest my head with oil; my cup overflows. Surely goodness and mercy shall follow me all the days of my life; and I shall dwell in the house of the Lord forever" (vv. 1, 5–6; cf. Num 4:7; Heb 9:2). All who humbly choose to come continuously to this Table receive lavish and overflowing grace in the midst of the world's evils, struggles, and tribulation.

164. Williams, *Being Christian*, 57–59.

165. White, *Sacraments as God's Self Giving*, 60. White proclaims: "[T]he Lord's Supper is an eschatological event, reaching ahead to the limits of time as well as back behind the beginning of time. God's self giving is not complete yet. The Eucharist is a foretaste of that which is yet to be. . . . We join the Christians of the New Testament in experiencing now the presence of the risen Lord and yet praying, 'Amen. Come, Lord Jesus!' (Rev 22:20)." Note that this precisely fits the purview of Scripture since the Last Supper was an immediate precursor to the Cross in *chronos*, yet the Lamb of God had already been slain in *kairos* before the chronological foundation of the world (Rev 13:8; cf. 1 Pet 1:20). The atonement makes possible and effective the coming Marriage Feast which will celebrate the divine culmination of existence. Thus, the present Lord's Supper (which administers an encounter with Christ) is soteriologically and cosmically eschatonic in

if they could presently view the unseen co-participants and the invisible theanthropic transaction that occurs (see Heb 12:18–24) at even the tiniest ecclesial gathering (Matt 18:20)! The Great I AM, who reigns as the King of the universe from the throne room of heaven, also stands on the earth amidst his worshipping people (Isa 66:1–2; Acts 7:48–50), drawing them near, offering his transformative grace, and caring for them (Pss 22:3; 113).[166]

The Theological Epilogue

In sacramental worship, God personally engages his people, lifts their hearts to his own heart, and embraces them in truth and love. Through the power of God, the worshipping church on earth is simultaneously and mysteriously participating in the divine worship of heaven.[167] This is what has been called in the Eastern church the "liturgy of ascension."[168] It is through this direct connection between God and the church that the Lord's Supper, combined with the proclamation of the Word, is the *principle* means by which the church receives the life-giving grace of God,[169] i.e., "the new life of the Kingdom," as appropriated through a "mustard seed's" modicum of

---

that it has foundation in the Last Supper (which announces the atonement of Christ) and fulfillment in the Wedding Supper (which announces the consummation of Christ). This means that when we engage in the *real presence* of the risen Christ at Holy Communion, we are effectually re-connected to the atonement and pre-connected to the consummation.

166. Purely as food for eschatological thought, could it be that the immediate (miniscule) time relationship in *chronos* between the Last Supper and the then-imminent atonement event (i.e., that time window described with such terms as "quickly"; "a little while"; "at once"—John 13:27, 31–33) is a similar proximity sign of the immediate time relationship in *kairos* between the Lord's Supper and the now-imminent consummation event (i.e., that time window described with such terms as "at hand"; "day"; "soon"—Jas 5:8; 2 Pet 3:8–10; Rev. 22:12)? Regardless, the fact of this indefinite (Matt 24:44), yet ever "soon" notion (for instance, see hymn: "He is Near," by Horatius Bonar and George C. Stebbins, 1896), should lend some significant degree of urgency and seriousness to our desire to be faithful in our Christian discipleship practices. After all, *chronos* will end—and with *eternal* ramifications.

167. Hahn, *Lamb's Supper*, 3, 56–57.

168. Schmemann, *For the Life*, 28.

169. Yrigoyen, *Praising the God of Grace*, 66–67.

seeking faith (Luke 17:5–6).[170] This is illustrated by the strong sacramental nature of Charles Wesley's lyrical theology:

> Savior, thou didst the mystery give
> That I thy nature might partake.
> Thou bidd'st me outward signs receive,
> One with myself thy soul to make,
> My body, soul and spi'rit join
> Inseparably one with thine.

> The prayer, the fast, the word conveys,
> When mixed with faith, thy life to me,
> In all the channels of thy grace,
> I still have fellowship with thee,
> But chiefly here my soul is fed
> With fullness of immortal bread.[171]

The Historical Foundation

> For John Wesley and classical Wesleyanism, tradition was [is] an authoritative source of religious truth . . . An understanding of the historic Christian tradition can guide us in distinguishing what is primary from what is secondary, what is culturally conditioned from what is of permanent character. The sacramental beliefs and practices of people through the centuries cannot be justifiably ignored.[172]

170. Witherington, *Making a Meal of it*, 136, 141–42. While stressing the importance of receiving both Word and Sacrament together (141), Witherington—following Charles Wesley—also declares the significance of the recipient's faith (136). Yet, note that even our *faith* is not self-induced, but of divine initiative and born of divine grace (Rom 12:3; cf. Eph 2:8–9; Rom 10:17; 1 Tim 1:13–14). Due to the grace of Christ in prevenience (i.e., "going before us"), *all* people ("every child of man," "every human heart") are given the enabling facility of *respondibility* to God (Wesley, "Heavenly Treasure in Earthen Vessels," 4:163), which can, through Word and Sacrament praxis, be first awakened and then developed and expanded with its continuous exercise (Wesley, "Earnest Appeal to Men," 11:77–79; also, see Oden, *Scriptural Christianity*, 243–47; Knight, *Presence of God*, 169–70; Phil 2:12–13; Crowe, *Church Health*, 131; cf. Wesley, "On Working Out," 3:199–209, but esp. 205–6). While, in faith, we are co-participative, God still gets all the glory.

171. Maddox, "Hymns," 39:54.3–4.

172. Staples, *Outward Sign*, 266.

The Primitive Origins of Word *and* Sacrament Worship

The premise that corporate Christian worship is centered in Word and Sacrament is not a recent understanding within Christianity. It goes back to the time of the apostolic church.[173] The aforementioned scriptural text of Acts 2:42 records what many scholars believe to be the earliest extant description of Christian worship (c. AD 80–115): "And they devoted themselves to the apostles' teaching and fellowship, to the breaking of bread and the prayers." Moreover, it is widely accepted among scholars that this text makes reference to the faithful practice of Word and Sacrament worship in the primitive church.[174]

Furthermore, an early extra-biblical source to describe Christian worship (AD 150) is found in Justin Martyr's classic, *The First Apology*.[175] Webber, in fact, considers this to be the earliest such non-canonical description.[176] Justin wrote, "And on the day called Sunday . . . the memoirs of the apostles or the writings of the prophets are read" and then "bread and wine and water are brought, and the president . . . offers prayers and thanksgivings . . . and the people assent, saying Amen; and there is a distribution to each."[177] This work patently substantiates the practice of regular Lord's Day Word and Sacrament in the Ante-Nicene church.[178]

Therefore, these two very early sources—one scriptural and one very early church patristic—clearly show evidence of Christian worship exemplifying Word and Sacrament praxis. Moreover, Ross affirms that Holy Communion "was very early joined with apostolic teaching" in worship pragmatics.[179] Likewise, Allmen asserts that "the [worship] rhythm, Word-

---

173. Martin, *Worship of God*, 203; Schaff, *Didache*, 27–28; Senn, *Stewardship of the Mysteries*, 5; Bradshaw, *Christian Worship*, 47–48.

174. Jeremias, *Eucharistic Words*, 115–122; Webber, *Worship Old & New*, 55; see also, Rattenbury, *Thoughts on Holy Communion*, 26–37.

175. Justin, "First Apology," 1:186; cf. Thompson, *Liturgies*, 3–10.

176. Webber, *Ancient-Future Worship*, 92.

177. Justin, "First Apology," 1:186.

178. Jourjon, "Justin," 71–77; LaVerdiere, *The Eucharist*, 178–79; Senn, *Stewardship of the Mysteries*, 5.

179. Ross, *Recalling the Hope of Glory*, 458. Additionally, other primitive Christian texts that highlight the regular worship practice of the Eucharist in the worship of the early Church include 1 Corinthians 10–11 (c. AD 53–54), Didache 9–10 (c. AD 50–150), and possibly 1 Clement 44:4 (c. AD 95–140).

Sacrament . . . is both that of the NT and of the first fifteen centuries."[180] This is significant, for as White emphasizes:

> The churches of the apostles and their immediate heirs have an authority for the Christian imagination that no other period can match. Golden age or not (1 Cor 11:29), all things liturgical are still tested by the standard of the earliest worshipping Christian communities.[181]

Without question, Wesley held this to be true.[182] In fact, he gave so much credence to the practices of the early church that he was given the nickname "Mr. Primitive Christianity."[183] Through his Anglican roots,[184] along with his array of other influences, and in particular from his studies of the primitive Acts church[185] and his reading of the Ante-Nicene Fathers,[186] Wesley came to understand the importance of Word and Sacrament praxis in the deepest possible way.[187] He knew that the very outward things that commonly signify the church as being the church—i.e., all good works of Christian love and compassion, the evangelistic mission of the church to seek and save the lost and to make disciples, etc., are actually overflows from the divine spiritual well of Word and Sacrament. Wesley—and the very functional fabric of his very distinctive working soteriology[188]—was indeed influenced by both the practices of the Acts church and the variant works of the early church fathers,[189] though always understood through the grid of Anglicanism.

180. Allmen, *Worship*, 286–87.

181. White, *Brief History*, 13.

182. Oh, *John Wesley's Ecclesiology*, 1–2, 9.

183. Baker, *John Wesley and the Church of England*, 34; Oh, *John Wesley's Ecclesiology*, 13.

184. Oh, *John Wesley's Ecclesiology*, 256.

185. Hildebrandt, *According to the Wesleys*, 47–49; Keefer, "Disciple of Early Christianity," 24–32; Payne, *American Methodism*, 16–17.

186. Baker, *John Wesley and the Church of England*, 33; Oh, *John Wesley's Ecclesiology*, 15; Oden, *John Wesley's Scriptural Christianity*, 65–69.

187. Wesley, "On the Church," 13:254. Note that Wesley was thoroughly familiar with the works of Justin Martyr. He had, in fact, translated Justin Martyr's *Apology*, which (as mentioned above) reveals the historic prominence of Word and Sacrament worship in the early church (see, Campbell, *John Wesley and Christian Antiquity*, 26).

188. For an excellent short essay on Wesley's ecumenical soteriology, see Collins, *Scripture Way of Salvation*, 205–7.

189. Although Wesley gave particular attention to the works of the Ante-Nicene

The Scriptural Church Context of Word *and* Sacrament Worship

As catholic and ecumenical-minded as he was, Wesley was indeed "a son of the church," that is, the Church of England.[190] His conception of the visible church was staunchly Anglican. He believed that the Church of England, even with its problems, was the most authentic modern manifestation of the scriptural church of Jesus Christ.[191] Throughout his entire life, Wesley held strongly and without deviation to Article XIX of the Church of England, which states: "The visible Church of Christ is a Congregation of faithful men [people], in which the pure Word of God is preached, and the Sacraments be duly administered according to Christ's Ordinance, in all those things that of necessity are requisite to the same."[192] Wesley's fervent desire to reform the Church of England was not because of any overt flaws in its inherent system and constitution, but rather due to a preponderance of "general spiritual lethargy" that had encompassed its constituency.[193] To Wesley, the system itself was not seriously broken; it just needed a spiritual reinvigoration among and within its practitioners.[194]

The core impetus of his Anglican ecclesiological understanding was a driving force for Wesley throughout the Methodist-Evangelical Revival. He believed without fail that faithful disciples were primarily formed and sustained by God through the efficacious practice of Constant Word and Sacrament.[195] Therefore, Wesley insisted that all members of Methodist societies faithfully participate in their local parish churches every Sunday because it was there that they would practice Word and Sacrament.[196] The ministry of

---

fathers, his patristic reading freely spanned the spectrum from Ante-Nicene to Nicene to Post-Nicene.

190. Baker, *John Wesley and the Church of England*, 7–21.

191. Oh, *John Wesley's Ecclesiology*, 60–61; Wood, *Meaning of Pentecost*, 155; cf. Wesley, "Letter to Dr. Coke," 13:252. Referring to the Church of England, he comments: "I think, the best constituted national Church in the world."

192. Oh, *John Wesley's Ecclesiology*, 256.

193. Walker, *History of the Christian Church*, 596.

194. Snyder, *Radical Wesley*, 72–73.

195. Felton, *This Holy Mystery*, 11; Willimon and Wilson, *Rekindling the Flame*, 113–14; Rattenbury, *Wesley's Legacy to the World*, 173–74.

196. See Spinks, "Anglicans and Dissenters," 521; cf. Wesley, "Thoughts upon Methodism," 9:527 (italics mine). Such a rudiment of basic Methodism has its origins in the earliest Holy Club days, of which Wesley wrote: "They were all zealous members of the Church of England, and had no particular opinions, but were distinguished only *by their constant attendance on church and Sacrament.*"

the Methodist societies, including the class meetings, was always intended to supplement, and not to replace, the ministry of the local church. The overarching purpose of the class meetings themselves was not primarily to teach Scripture and theology, but to ensure through accountability, encouragement, and support, that the members were staying consistently true in their growth as disciples of Jesus Christ.[197] The class meetings became a sure way, as Wesley said, to "watch over the souls of their brethren."[198] As indicated by Watson, in a real sense, it is not incorrect to say that the class meetings and their leaders served as the "spiritual police" of Methodism.[199] They provided spiritual oversight.

Thus, the class meetings were designed to help keep the members walking along the straight and narrow Christian path and to hold them true to their commitment to God. Yet, their supernatural empowerment to actually be able to fulfill that walk and commitment came from God through their ongoing and faithful practice of the Instituted means of grace,[200] including, most importantly, their regular attendance of Lord's

197. See Watson, *Early Methodist Class Meeting*, 97–98. There was certainly an ongoing cadre of renegade Methodist associates who felt that the circuit preaching was all that was necessary and thereby tried to disaffiliate themselves from the local parish churches. Of course, dealing with these types of matters was part of the purpose of the class meetings.

198. Wesley, "Thoughts upon Methodism," 9:529; cf. Watson, *Early Methodist Class Meeting*, 93.

199. Watson, *Early Methodist Class Meeting*, 101.

200. In the Wesleyan understanding, the Instituted means of grace (those "instituted" directly by Jesus Christ himself) included Holy Communion, Holy Scripture ("searching the Scriptures"), Holy Conference ("Christian conference"), Holy Prayer, and Holy Fasting. Note that the class meetings themselves were considered to be a Prudential (or prudently useful) means of grace (see Watson, *Early Methodist Class Meeting*, 93; cf. Knight, *Presence of God*, 5), but notably not an Instituted means of grace (although we suggest that small group gatherings, like class meetings, can conceivably be considered to be a variation of Holy Conference). While the categories of Instituted means of grace are limited to the above five, the Prudential means of grace are rather open ended and could include any Christian means that are prudent to the practice and development of Christian faith and faithfulness, but usually with a special focus on the outward social practices of compassion, peace, justice, and mercy. Often, the Prudential means are related to the *Three General Rules* (do no harm; do only good; attend upon all the ordinances of God) (see Harper, *Prayer & Devotional Life*, 34). Interestingly, including the ordinances as a Prudential means presents a very significant overlap with the Instituted means, which shows Wesley's extreme and primary emphasis on the need for holiness of heart in order to fulfill holiness of life. Furthermore, it should also be noted that Wesley believed God, in fact, could use *anything* as a means of grace, or even *nothing* at all (see Wesley, "Means of Grace," 1:382). However, he taught that there were certain things that

Day local parish worship, with its central focus being on Word and Sacrament. From the very beginning, Methodism was designed "not to form any new sect," but rather to help the established church become renewed and focused in its mission of being and making disciples.[201] For Wesley, Constant Word and Sacrament praxis was the functional foundation and power tool of fulfilling that objective.[202]

The Extraordinary Provisions for Word *and* Sacrament Worship

This understanding is perhaps demonstrated in no greater way than by the extraordinary efforts of Wesley to ensure the ongoing continuity of Word and Sacrament opportunity and practice among the Methodist societies in Britain and America. Wesley was compelled, even driven, to make sacramental provision for all Methodists and to implore all Methodists toward their duty to participate constantly.[203] This became most apparent in 1783 with the conclusion of the Revolutionary War. It was then that a new sacramental crisis came to pass among the Methodists in America.

The matter of the Sacraments—both the issue of their accessibility to the Methodist people in general and the issue of their administration by Methodist preachers—was something that Wesley had thought much about over the course of many years.[204] However, in the period of 1783–84, with the new post-Revolution situation in America, inclusive of the exit of the Church of England from the colonies, there developed an ongoing condition of increasingly extreme urgency. American Methodists had been

---

God had chosen to ordinarily use. It is those very things by which we would do well to spiritually and pragmatically indulge ourselves.

201. Wesley, "Minutes of Several Conversations," 8:299. This is written in Wesley's "Large Minutes": "Q.3. What may we reasonably believe to be God's design in raising up the Preachers called Methodists? A. Not to form any new sect; but to reform the nation, particularly the Church; and to spread scriptural holiness over the land" (299).

202. See Rattenbury, *Wesley's Legacy to the World*, 174, where he strongly asserts, "The Methodist Movement was not only a missionary appeal to outsiders, but a revival of devotional, and especially sacramental, practice in the Church of England. The Wesleys, with all their fervid evangelicalism, never ceased to be sacramentalists, and there is no antithesis more false than the common one of Sacrament and gospel. The Wesleys found the Lord's Supper a source of evangelical power"; cf. Snyder, *Radical Wesley*, 74.

203. Wesley, "Duty of Constant Communion," 3:428–29.

204. Norwood, *Story of American Methodism*, 96.

deserted by their Anglican clergy brethren and had thus become largely devoid of sacramental opportunity.

Prior to this, the Methodist situation had not been so dire. The American societies engaged with the local Anglican congregations in Lord's Day worship and Sacraments. There had been no overt need for Methodists to have to administer the Sacraments themselves. Methodism could remain focused on its primary mission of proclamational evangelism. Theologically, the primary Methodist ministry of lay preaching was justified by Wesley in his separation of the offices of pastor and evangelist. In fact, he believed it to be "a return to New Testament practice."[205]

In Wesley's understanding, the office of pastor was an ordinary ministry of preaching, pastoral care, and sacramental administration. Such ordinary ministry required episcopal ordination. However, Methodist preachers were not pastors. They practiced the office of evangelist and thus carried out an extraordinary ministry that did not include the ordinary ministry duties of pastoral care and sacramental administration. Such ministry did not require episcopal ordination.[206] Yet, when the Anglican departure occurred, the scenario drastically changed. In effect, American Methodism went from being a *church within the church* (*ecclesiolae in ecclesia*) to being a disconnected parachurch organization without ordained clergy and without accessibility to ordained clergy (for sacramental administration). This brought Wesley out of necessity to a point of major ecclesiological decision.

Since Wesley was a sacerdotalist (making either independent self-ordination or lay administration of the Sacraments out of the question), his only choice was to provide for some manner of valid ordination.[207] Under the influence of his readings of Lord Peter King[208] and Edward Stillingfleet,[209] Wesley had long before concluded that his priestly orders sufficed him with the authority to ordain.[210] He had come to believe that the biblical terms of *bishop* and *presbyter* were, in fact, synonymous,[211] and

205. Snyder, *Radical Wesley*, 93.

206. Payne, *American Methodism*, 6–7; Snyder, *Radical Wesley*, 91–94.

207. Norwood, *Story of American Methodism*, 96.

208. Wesley, "Journal" (January 20, 1746), 2:6–7; Wesley, "Letter to Dr. Coke," 13:251. For further, see King, *Enquiry into the Constitution*.

209. Wesley, "Letter to his Brother Charles," 12:147. For further, see Stillingfleet, *Irenicum*.

210. Norwood, *Sourcebook of American Methodism*, 80, 82.

211. Wesley, "Scripture Way of Salvation," 2:6–7.

therefore he was actually a "scriptural *episcopos*," even if not an Anglican *episcopos*.[212]

In light of this reasoning, and as a pragmatic matter of extraordinary necessity, Wesley then finally acted and proceeded to ordain Richard Whatcoat and Thomas Vasey as "elders" with sacramental authority.[213] He also "set apart" Thomas Coke as a general superintendent with the power to ordain.[214] These men were then sent by Wesley from Britain to the American Methodists in order to provide for their needed sacramental relief. Upon arrival, Whatcoat and Vasey could immediately begin administering the Sacraments, and Coke could immediately begin ordaining other Methodist preachers to take sacramental authority. This was the final act of Wesley that led to the official formation of the Methodist Episcopal Church. As Wesley wrote somewhat prophetically in the final words of his letter to "Our Brethren in North America":

> As our American brethren are now totally disentangled both from the State, and from the English hierarchy, we dare not entangle them again, either with the one or the other. They are now at full liberty, simply to follow the Scriptures and the primitive Church. And we judge it best that they should stand fast in the liberty wherewith God has so strangely made them free.[215]

With the spirit and authority of these words, the Christmas Conference of 1784, held at Lovely Lane Chapel in Baltimore, Maryland, took their full liberty and formed the Methodist Episcopal Church. On three successive days, Coke ordained Asbury first to deacon, then to elder, and finally to general superintendent.[216] They then followed with the ordination of either twelve or thirteen Methodist lay preachers (the exact number is not known) to the ministerial office of elder with full sacramental authority.[217] As such, Wesley's American revival child had grown into a fully independent ecclesial adult. Wesley had successfully and fully completed in an extraordinary

212. Norwood, *Story of American Methodism*, 96.

213. Norwood, *Sourcebook of American Methodism*, 79; Wesley, "Journal" (September 1, 1784), 4:288.

214. Wesley, "Letter to Dr. Coke," 13:251–52.

215. Wesley, "Letter to Dr. Coke," 13:252.

216. For an entertaining letter (dated September 20, 1788) from Wesley to Asbury "scorching" him and Coke for altering their titles from general superintendent to bishop, see Norwood, *Sourcebook of American Methodism*, 98–99.

217. Norwood, *Story of American Methodism*, 100–1.

manner the functional bequeathal to the American Methodists of the two pillars of his missional ecclesiology: Word and Sacrament.[218]

The Historical Epilogue

The words of Wesley and his actions were a decisive statement about his staunch convictions as to the true pillars of the church; yet his actions spoke still louder than even his words. He spent much of himself through the constant innovation of new and extraordinary ways to both propagate the proclamation of the Word of God (e.g., through the implementation of lay preachers [including women!], open-air preaching, itineration, etc.) and to ensure that the people of God had constant accessibility to the necessary Sacraments of God (e.g., through the implementation of scriptural *episcopos* ordinations, the granting of freedom to form a new ecclesial institution, etc.). Though Wesley did his best to honor the precepts and institutional parameters of the Church of England, he understood that the mission of God to advance the cause of Christ superseded all other things.[219] Where the institution stood as a hindrance to the fulfillment of the scriptural soteriological mission, it was at that point precisely that the institution required a necessary practical abrogation.

For Wesley, everything—whether theological or practical—was really about the church fulfillment of the Christian *soteriological* mission to make disciples of Jesus Christ.[220] And yet at its very constitution, Wesley's

218. In his "Letter to Dr. Coke, Mr. Asbury, and Our Brethren in North America," note that Wesley spoke not only of providing for the necessity of "Traveling Preachers," but also of his provision of "a Liturgy, little differing from that of the Church of England," as well as his advisement for "the Elders to administer the supper of the Lord on every Lord's day" (13:251–52). The provision for Constant Word and Sacrament worship remained ever his priority.

219. Wesley, "Letter to Dr. Coke." Wesley emphasized: "I was determined as little as possible to violate the established order of the national Church to which I belonged." Yet, the extraordinary sacramental necessity of the Gospel prevailed and finally forced his hand; he said: "my scruples are at an end" (252).

220. Wesley, "Large Minutes," 10:854: "You have nothing to do but save souls. Therefore spend and be spent in this work"; cf. Wood, *Burning Heart*, 84; also, Coleman, *Nothing to Do*. Coleman asserts: "The mandate of Christ is not to make converts, but to 'make disciples'—followers of Jesus—persons who will develop into the likeness of the Master . . . John Wesley focused this strategy of the Great Commission in his charge to the preachers, not only to bring sinners to repentance, but 'to build them up in that holiness without which they cannot see the Lord'" (79–80). For further, see Knight, *Presence of God*, 1–2: "Unquestionably, John Wesley's central concern was the Christian life. . . . His

missional ecclesiology remained ultimately fixed upon those two mighty pillars set absolutely and uncompromisingly in historic Anglican stone: Word and Sacrament.[221] For Wesley, the central place of Word and Sacrament and the salvific mission of the church were in perfect conjunctive harmony with one another. For Wesley, sinners became disciples under the superintendence of the Holy Spirit through the constant praxis of Word and Sacrament. For Wesley, all else—every ministry innovation, every missional adaptation of his practical divinity—extended from or devised from those two pillars which are connected inseparably as one. As Wesley demonstrated, the praxis of Word and Sacrament is the essence of the visible church of Jesus Christ and the very center of all Christian mission. It was the understanding of Wesley that such had been the case, at least, since the birth of the primitive, apostolic church.

The Conclusion

This chapter has presented compelling arguments from multiple perspectives as to the necessity of Constant Word and Sacrament praxis. The arguments from biblical, theological, and historical foundations have strongly demonstrated the connection of the practice with the church from apostolic to modern times. It also points to the current need for the widespread application of Wesleyan sacramentalism across all of United Methodism. This is deemed to be essential for authentic and efficacious Christian worship and to ultimately fulfill the mission of making disciples of Jesus Christ for the transformation of the world.

In the next chapter, we will integrate some contemporary thinking with classic Wesleyan precepts. This will be done in order to show how certain recent postulations may have positive impact upon the use of Constant Word and Sacrament in the disciple-making ministry of today's local United Methodist churches.

---

evangelistic ministry was a passionate affirmation that this new life was offered to all; his pastoral ministry involved the patient nurture and direction of those who sought to grow in this life. Certainly no treatment of Wesley's theology can long avoid an examination of the soteriology which lies at its heart" (1).

221. In August 1785 (late in his life), referring to Article XIX of the Church of England (i.e., the *Word + Sacrament = Church* article), Wesley affirmingly commented: "Here is a true logical definition, containing both the essence and the properties of a church" (Wesley, "Letter to Dr. Coke," 13:254).

3

The Contemporary Foundations

For better or for worse, a large segment of Protestantism has remained in the orbit of the Enlightenment in its sacramental life.
Strong suspicion remains with regard to the union of the physical
and the spiritual . . . Sacraments are seen largely in a moralistic
framework, reminding us of the past work of Christ but rarely
seen as a present encounter with him today . . . This was not the
strain of John Wesley and the early Methodists. In a countercultural mode, they found the Sacraments gracious forms of encounter with Christ . . . But through a long process in the nineteenth
century, this sacramental edge was gradually lost in Methodism,
and enlightenment ideas prevailed instead of John Wesley's rich
sacramental life.[1]

WE HAVE REVIEWED THE biblical, theological, and historical foundations
for the classic Wesleyan praxis of Constant Word and Sacrament in the
worship life of the local United Methodist church, and despite the diminu-
tion of its regard today as posited by White above, we have found strong
justification in all three areas for its continued or renewed usage. In this
chapter, we will turn to the works of some pertinent contemporary writers
and ascertain how their ideas and postulations may have impact on the
current application of the concept.

The plan is as follows. In the first section (Contemporary Situation),
we will discuss the present (bleak) sacramental scenario within the United

1. White, *Sacraments in Protestant Practice*, 22–23.

Methodist Church and suggest the need for pragmatic change. In the second section (Contemporary Solution), we will discuss some contemporary thoughts on fulfilling the Christian mission and relate them to Constant Word and Sacrament praxis in the local church. Finally, in the third section (Contemporary Application), we will then propose a practical application for the reformation and recovery of Wesleyan sacramental spirituality within United Methodism, especially as it pertains to the local church's fulfillment of its mission to make disciples of Jesus Christ.

The Contemporary Situation

> United Methodism is at a critical crossroads. Forces within the culture and the denomination are pushing toward secularism. In an effort to remain in homeostasis with a changing society, the denomination is allowing the society to change its core identity. United Methodism no longer reflects the ideals or corporate culture of Wesley or EAM [Early American Methodism]. It has become the establishment.[2]

In the words of Payne, United Methodism "has become the establishment."[3] What then have we become? As American society identifies more and more with values and understandings predicated strongly on such Enlightenment-derived ideologies as secularism, naturalism, empiricism, pluralism, and humanism, it becomes more and more overtly antagonistic to the exclusive biblical presentation of Christian theism. Thus, in order to remain relevant in a changing world, many parts of the church are actually giving up, perhaps both consciously and unconsciously, portions of its distinctive Christian identity. Rather than standing against the tide as a bastion of supernatural biblical truth and thus an agent of societal reform, in order to survive and be accepted, the church has instead accommodated the establishment and, as such, is dispossessing itself of certain elements of its divine character and nature. Astoundingly, the visible church itself seems to be moving deeply into a form of spiritual post-Christianism. In many ways, Vahanian, in his impactful book *The Death of God* (2011), is quite prescient, even oracular. He states:

---

2. Payne, *American Methodism*, 254.

3. Payne, *American Methodism*, 254.

Unfortunately, Christianity is too intimately, even inextricably, bound up with patterns and structures which hav[e] become secularized . . . An organized Christianity [think Payne, above: the Church "has become the establishment"] does not simulate the patterns of the spirit. . . . [which] can be distinguished from those of the world. . . . To contrast the two, one can say that the patterns of the spirit are prophetic, while those of the world and those of an organization are institutional or tradition-bound. The prophetic spirit does not deny the world and its traditions or its organizations. It even makes use of them. But it does not wed itself to them. Nor does it enslave them. Were it to do so, the prophetic spirit would lose its own identity, its own authenticity.[4]

This is precisely what has been, and is, happening. As the church weds itself to the world, it diminishes the vitality of the prophetic Spirit and becomes functionally moribund. God is not really dead, but in copious corners of the church, people are practicing their "faith" as if he is. A widespread mindset where God is not being treated as providential, transcendent, and sacramental is strong testament to this. For example, Vahanian asserts that true Christian faith demands "the conversion of our human reality, both culturally and existentially."[5] Yet, as Payne observes, this actuality of conversion is not radically present within, nor radically mediated by, current United Methodism in America.[6]

Today, many people and many congregations of the United Methodist Church have rejected the biblical notion of an active supernaturalism and have thus functionally abdicated the premise of classic sacramental theology.[7] White observes, "sacramental practice has for many Protestants become a marginal part of their religious life."[8] As such, while maintaining much lip service to the power and presence of the divine and the high authority and inspiration of Holy Scripture, Davis contends that we have functionally given up significant aspects of the majestic concept of God in favor of a much lesser, false deity.[9] Meanwhile, Webber is correct when he

---

4. Vahanian, *Death of God*, 10.

5. Vahanian, *Wait Without Idols*, 46.

6. Payne, *American Methodism*, 254.

7. White, *Sacraments in Protestant Practice*, 22–23.

8. White, *Sacraments in Protestant Practice*, 23.

9. Davis, *Worship and the Reality*, 37–40.

asserts that a "steady march toward a new anti-supernatural faith is already evident in worship and spirituality."[10] He further elaborates:

> This divorce of worship and spirituality from God's story of creation, incarnation, and re-creation has resulted in a new kind of Gnostic worship and spirituality. The denial of a consistent supernaturalism in which God is disclosed not only in Jesus and in Scripture but also at bread and wine is a clash of vision. To say that God is not communicated to us through visible and tangible signs such as gatherings of people, the words of Scripture, and the material reality of water, bread, and wine is a rejection of creation as the handiwork of God. Ultimately, if carried to its conclusion, this view will reject that God was united to human flesh in the incarnation. The mystery of faith embraces the reality of the incarnation and an incarnational presence in the bread and wine.[11]

Unfortunately, a non-sacramental and non-incarnational understanding of church and worship is a tragic ecclesial reality that is played out every Lord's Day in many United Methodist congregations. Davis provides this summation:

> In practice, it seems that ordinary evangelical Protestant concepts of the church reflect notions that are more sociological than theological, more functional and pragmatic than "mystical" and ontological, more Pelagian than Pauline and pneumatic—that is, an eviscerated ecclesiology in which the church is viewed [merely] as a voluntary human organization gathered for certain activities: worship and praise, instruction and motivation, and friendship.[12]

Borgen concurs with Davis; in fact, he describes the contemporary spiritual *ethos* of Methodism as "self-sufficient, middle-class, work righteousness."[13] Therefore, since many United Methodists have unwarily slipped into a form of Pelagianism,[14] they miss "the Church's entrance into heaven" in their worship and, as such, default from a regular immersion into the new life of Christ and his kingdom.[15]

---

10. Webber, *Ancient-Future Worship*, 135.

11. Webber, *Ancient-Future Worship*, 135.

12. Davis, *Worship and the Reality*, 63.

13. Borgen, *John Wesley on the Sacraments*, 282.

14. Borgen, *John Wesley on the Sacraments*, 281–82; also, Davis, *Worship and the Reality*, 63.

15. Schmemann, *Eucharist*, 27; *For the Life*, 28.

The postulations of Webber, Borgen, Davis, and White are indicators that contemporary United Methodism, unlike with Wesley and the early Methodists, has become an entity heavily dependent on anthropocentric thought and endeavor and largely devoid of supernaturalistic expectation and empowerment. In our deviation from a strong eucharistic theology and its corresponding Word and Sacrament practice in our local churches, we have in effect, rejected Wesley's "full, rich and joyous eucharistic life," of which, according to Chilcote, "there is no question" drove the Methodist-Evangelical Revival.[16] As such, Khoo also identifies the catalyst of the revival event when she describes it specifically as "a *eucharistic* revival."[17] One worship entity—God's Table administered, always preceded by God's Word proclaimed—was and still is the key power practice of missional Methodism. It is the main incendiary point for life-giving Holy Spirit action.

Wesley saw many similarities in the practices and movement of the Acts 2 church and those of the Methodist Revival. To apply the description from White (and Chilcote, above), both indeed shared that "rich sacramental life."[18] As shown in the last chapter, the Acts church, centered in Word and Sacrament, exploded with the power of God and manifested itself in the salvation of many souls. In fact, "John Wesley was profoundly influenced by this idea" of Word and Sacrament centrality in the early church.[19] In the Evangelical Revival, Wesley and his fellow Methodists perceived themselves to be in a matching pattern with the primitive church [20] and the agents of a new Pentecost.[21]

In *American Methodism: Past & Future Growth* (2013), Payne concurs with White and Chilcote in that Methodism "intuitively understood this [early church] process because it duplicated it" and in so doing "was

16. Chilcote, *Recapturing the Wesleys' Vision*, 84–85; also, see Rattenbury, *Thoughts on Holy Communion*, 7. Here he affirms: "Methodists possess a great eucharistic tradition. Indeed it is not improper to describe the Evangelical Revival as also a sacramental revival."

17. Khoo, *Wesleyan Eucharistic Spirituality*, 73 (italics mine). She says: "Something happened at the table. That was why there was a eucharistic revival."

18. White, *Sacraments in Protestant Practice*, 23; cf. Chilcote, *Recapturing the Wesleys' Vision*, 84.

19. Chilcote, *Recapturing the Wesleys' Vision*, 80.

20. Payne, *American Methodism*, 16–17.

21. Wesley, "Journal (October 28, 1762)," 21:392. Note that Wesley wrote, "Many years ago my brother frequently said, 'Your day of Pentecost is not fully come. But I doubt not it will, and you will then hear of persons sanctified as frequently as you do now of persons justified.' Any unprejudiced reader may observe that it is now fully come."

a disciple-making machine that modeled the evangelistic ideal of the New Testament."[22] Conversely, as contemporary Methodism has moved away from its centering in Constant Word and Sacrament praxis, the power of God has become much less visibly and demonstratively explosive and the salvation of souls has diminished in plentitude.[23] This makes sense, for as Felton strongly emphasizes, both Word *and* Sacrament contribute to the potency of the church's mission:

> Encounter with the living Christ at the Table transforms people and empowers them for the ministry of evangelism. . . . sacramentalism and evangelism have sometimes been considered in opposition to each other. This idea is a distortion of the gospel message and particularly, of the teaching and practice of John Wesley. Participation in the Sacraments is one of the most potent ways by which people are imbued with the imperative to engage in evangelism. The Sacraments are not chiefly ends in themselves; they are means to enable the church to continue Christ's ministry of redeeming the world.[24]

Word and Sacrament live and breathe as one. A lack of Word and Sacrament praxis in the church translates into a lack of effective evangelism by the church and thus a diminishment of participation by the church in "Christ's ministry of redeeming the world."[25] In contrast to both the church of Acts 2, which "added to their number day by day those that were being saved" (Acts 2:47), and to the early Methodists who surged across Britain and America and "spread scriptural holiness over the land,"[26] contemporary United Methodism has veritably abated in general numbers every year since its formation in 1968.[27] Despite the excuses sometimes given to

22. Payne, *American Methodism*, 17.

23. This, of course, should be expected because, as Oden emphasizes, "there can be no church without a fitting sacramental life" (Oden, *Classic Christianity*, 718). See also, Rattenbury, *Eucharistic Hymns*, 255–56 (Hymn 166, esp. stanzas four and eleven). In this hymn, Charles Wesley attributes the pervasive weakness of the later church to the widespread cessation of Constant Holy Communion.

24. Felton, *This Holy Mystery*, 55; cf. Rattenbury, *Wesley's Legacy to the World*, 174, where he states: "The Wesleys found the Lord's Supper a source of evangelical power."

25. Felton, *This Holy Mystery*, 55.

26. Wesley, "Minutes of Several Conversations," 8:299.

27. Actually, the Methodist Church, prior to the merger with the EUB Church in 1968 to form the UMC, had already begun to show a membership decline at least as early as 1964. In fact, between 1964 and 1968, the pre-UMC abatement went from a peak of 11,054,634 members to 10,955,610 (Wilke, *And are We Yet Alive?*, 16). Since

justify, or even to deny or dismiss, this demise, there is really nothing good to be said for it. Quite pungently, Wilke likens this slow death condition to "a faint rustling of shrouds."[28] The bottom line is that, overall, United Methodism in America is not growing quantitatively.[29]

Moreover, aside from the continued year-to-year reduction in sheer numerical strength, United Methodism has also lost its prior countercultural edge. It has become less and less transforming of society and more and more accommodating to the secular environment.[30] Again, we believe that this is significantly related to a general departure from our Wesleyan roots in eucharistic theology and worship. Felton explains the significance of Methodist sacramentalism:

> The Sacraments are God's gifts to the gathered body of believers to form the church into Christ's body in ministry to the world. Through Holy Communion, the Holy Spirit works to shape our moral and ethical lives. In the ongoing process of conversion, we grow in personal and social holiness and are empowered to work for healing, compassion, reconciliation, justice, and peace. . . . The United Methodist Church has a heritage from John Wesley in which ethical discipleship was inextricably related to sacramental worship.[31]

Over time, Methodism has separated itself from this Wesleyan heritage. To apply Felton's postulation, our contemporary disregard for sacramental worship has led to a severe decrease in conversion, sanctification, and ethical discipleship development. The result is that United Methodism is not even notably making converts, let alone notably making disciples of Jesus Christ for the transformation of the world. As Payne asserts, this is in direct contrast to the divine will because "God wants the church to make

---

the 1968 merger, The United Methodist Church has continued its annual decline to a current 2015 membership of 7,067,162; note that the 2014 membership was 7,299,753, indicating a loss of 232,591 members in just the most recent data year (www.umc.org/gcfa/data-services).

28. Wilke, *And Are We Yet Alive?*, 66.

29. Note that these are overall numbers. Both Schaller (*Ice Cube is Melting*, 28–47) and Payne (*American Methodism*, 21–49) indicate a lack of uniformity in the numbers. This means that there are regions within America that have shown signs of growth during certain periods of time, but broadly speaking, the American connection as a whole has shown nothing but numerical loss for decades.

30. Payne, *American Methodism*, 254.

31. Felton, *This Holy Mystery*, 56.

disciples."[32] United Methodism in America overall is currently growing neither quantitatively (in sheer numbers) nor qualitatively (in depth and degree of Christian discipleship and in societal impact).

Payne makes a powerful case that both kinds of growth are imperative. This is because quantitative and qualitative growth are correlative to one another and both are signs of spiritual health. Consistently increasing numbers can be a strong indicator that God is at work and that evangelism and deepening discipleship are occurring in and through the church.[33] Payne presents some striking statistics that show the growth and subsequent societal influence of Early American Methodism (EAM). For instance, in 1790, 18.5 percent of the U.S. population was affiliated with the Methodist Episcopal Church. By 1840, that number had further increased to an astounding 56.9 percent.[34] Such an incredible numerical growth had a powerful transforming influence on general society. As Payne explains:

> In truth, it made a big difference. In EAM, affiliation led to spiritual maturity and right living. The discipleship process included a deep conviction of sin, awakening, repentance, personal faith in Christ, participation in a local class [Methodist class meeting], keeping the discipline, accountability, and the regular use of the various means of grace. As Methodists "moved toward perfection," they underwent a radical change. Furthermore, as the membership increased, the social sway of EAM on the emerging American ethos also increased. By 1810, the transforming influence from Methodism's growing tentacles reached deep into the political and cultural arenas of American life.[35]

Payne adds further, concerning the implications:

> Granted, numerical growth for the sake of more people in the pews is of little value unless the growth is related to a larger process of salvation, discipleship, and transformation. If American Methodism were reinvigorated so that it took on the character and soul of

---

32. Payne, *American Methodism*, ix.

33. Please understand that it is not about increasing numbers for the sake of having impressive statistics. It is about seeking and saving the lost (cf. Luke 19:10) and remembering that each number represents a precious eternal soul who is a seeker or a convert and a potential disciple of Jesus Christ.

34. Payne, *American Methodism*, 3.

35. Payne, *American Methodism*, 4.

EAM, it would become a potent force for spiritual vitality, social holiness, and apostolic faith.[36]

Contemporary United Methodism is in dire need of such a reinvigoration. The fruit of "salvation, discipleship, and transformation," or rather the lack thereof, does not lie. Hamilton concurs:

> We don't often use the word *revival* anymore. For many, the idea of revival is quaint at best; at worst, it calls up images of tent meetings where silver-tongued preachers take advantage of gullible believers. But the word, based on the Latin *re-vivere*, means to reinvigorate, to restore to life, to become strong and healthy after a period of decline, to renew or revitalize. . . . [C]hurches, denominations, and even revival movements within the Christian faith . . . [can] . . . eventually lose their vitality. Even in the New Testament period, the writer of the Book of Revelation noted that some of the churches in Asia had lost their "first love" and become "lukewarm." The same might be said of the denominational families that sprang out of the Wesleyan movement. I believe the seeds

---

36. Payne, *American Methodism*, 4. Please note Payne's (and Felton's, above) proper use of the term "social holiness" as opposed to "social justice." The two terms are not correctly interchangeable. *Social holiness* has a distinctly scriptural basis in the Great Commandment and, by extension, is found in the Wesleyan concept of holiness of heart (loving God) leading to holiness of life (loving others). Meanwhile, *social justice* is a more general term that can conceivably be used in a Christian context, yet is often epistemologically claimed from any number of variant perspectival milieus, many of which are secular and non-Christian (and sometimes even antithetical to the Christian faith and salvific mission). In a word, social justice—not being distinctively Christian—involves efforts of various motivations to fix diverse forms of perceived injustice inherent within the social order of this fallen world. Contrastingly, in the Wesleyan tradition, social holiness—being distinctively Christian—involves the process whereby God is restoring our marred divine image and providing for our sanctification unto perfection in and through the church which exists within the social order of this fallen world. (There can be no holiness apart from God-in-Christ.) The core of social holiness is this: Christ, through his sanctified church, is advancing the kingdom of God and its holy ethos. In social holiness, as Payne rightly stresses (above), the church first becomes changed by the sanctifying power of Christ and then becomes an agent of Christ-empowered "salt and light" as a consequence (think Wesley's notion: "To reform the nation, particularly the church, and to spread scriptural holiness over the land"). Social justice operates primarily with a focus on generic human equality and concomitant rights; social holiness operates primarily with a focus on Christian transformational soteriology and concomitant practiced discipleship. While there can seem to be some functional overlap, the two concepts should not be conflated.

of our revival, and the revival of Christianity today, are to be found in the story of our beginning.[37]

Following this thought of Hamilton, "the story of our [Methodist] beginning" is filled with revival and transformation.[38] Wesley and the early Methodists were concerned about their own transformation and discipleship growth so that they could become God's agents of wider transformation and the makers of other disciples. In its most basic and purest expression, Methodism has always been tantamount to a ministry of *transformational* revivalism and rampant social *holiness*. Wesley's own description of Methodism's transformational reason for being was simple and direct: "To reform the nation, especially the church, and to spread scriptural holiness over the land."[39] Stetzer and Rainer essentially recapitulate Wesley's heart:

> TRANSFORMATION + CHURCH . . . For Followers of Jesus, these are two of the most important and powerful words in the world. We treasure the concept of "transformation" because radical change is the heart of the Christian message and because the power of the gospel changes everything – lives, churches, and communities. [Furthermore] Christians love "church" because God has chosen the community of Christ followers to make known His manifest wisdom (Eph 3:10). When God transforms lives, He doesn't just build temples of the Holy Spirit in individuals, He builds His church by adding more lives to the body. God uses individuals in the church to bring about the transformation of more individuals and, consequently, the growth of the church. The church is God's tool and instrument for His kingdom agenda.[40]

We notice their observation that divine transformation affects not only individuals, but also impacts local churches, whole communities, and the wider expansion of the greater kingdom of God. Further, Stetzer and Rainer present this admonition:

> The truth is that transformation is non-negotiable for the Christian church. But change is not the norm for many of our churches. We are supposed to see transformation, but too often we see stagnation. God's plan is that "We all, with unveiled faces, are reflecting the glory of the Lord and are being transformed into

---

37. Hamilton, *Revival*, 11–12.
38. Hamilton, *Revival*, 12.
39. Wesley, "Minutes of Several Conversations," 8:299.
40. Stetzer and Rainer, *Transformational Church*, 1.

the same image from glory to glory; this is from the Lord who is the Spirit" (2 Cor 3:18). That means that we (as individuals) and "we all" (as the church) are supposed to see this transformation. Transforming from glory to glory should be normal, but too often it is exceptional.[41]

The church is the God-chosen instrument to change the world. Thus, transformation is the church's biblical imperative (2 Cor 3:18). Yet, as Stetzer and Rainer posit, the making of disciples and the transforming of the world has actually become the ecclesial exception and no longer the rule.[42] This has certainly become the case for United Methodism. Our spiritual and missional revitalization is critically needed.

The Contemporary Solution

[T]he healthiest churches in America tended to have a simple process for making disciples. They had clarity about the process. They moved Christians intentionally through the process. They were focused on the elements of the process. And they aligned their entire congregation to this process. [Thus] The simple church was discovered.[43]

In recent years, we have been inundated with a seemingly endless number of books proposing theoretical solutions to enhance the effectiveness of the church and its ministry. In my circles, the most prominent ones include such works as Rick Warren's *The Purpose-Driven Church* (1995), Robert Schnase's *Five Practices of Fruitful Congregations* (2007), and Scott J. Jones and Bruce R. Ough's *Seven Vision Pathways* (2010).[44] There is no doubt

41. Stetzer and Rainer, *Transformational Church*, 2.

42. Stetzer and Rainer, *Transformational Church*, 2.

43. Rainer and Geiger, *Simple Church*, ix.

44. Additionally, a few years back, Bishop Al Gwinn (then, the resident bishop of the Raleigh, North Carolina Area) also recommended that the clergy of the NCC read a secular bestseller by Jim Collins called *Good to Great* (2001). This book is about the common practices shared by several very successful companies which, in Gwinn's estimation, could possibly be applied to the church institution. Interestingly, Chip Ingram—in somewhat of a spin-off of Collins' work—wrote a distinctively Christian treatise called *Good to Great in God's Eyes* (2007). Ingram bills his book as "ten practices great Christians have in common." Both are excellent in their own right and, with proper appropriation, can contribute positively to kingdom work. Yet, as do the three books mentioned above, both of these share certain potentially daunting applicative complexities.

that each of these formulations (and others) has and will continue to commend themselves well to the work of the kingdom. Each of them is an honorable effort to advance the cause of Christ in and through his holy church. Each of them offers wisdom and has their place. The first two above are directed specifically at the local church. The third is more denominationally directed.

Warren advocates that a local church should be purpose driven. In his paradigm, this is accomplished by following a five-part church growth strategy that Warren avers was originated in the ministry of Jesus. A local church grows warmer through fellowship. A local church grows deeper through discipleship. A local church grows stronger through worship. A local church grows broader through ministry. A local church grows larger through evangelism.[45] Each of his five purposes have biblical validity; yet, there are still five.

Schnase meanwhile takes the very Wesleyan-biblical image of fruitfulness and applies it to the local congregation. According to this model, a local congregation will thrive as they faithfully practice the following: radical hospitality, passionate worship, intentional faith development, risk-taking mission and service, and extravagant generosity.[46] Each of his five practices also has biblical validity; yet again, there are five emphases.

Jones and Ough take a much broader United Methodist denominational approach. This model provides seven pathways to follow, each of which falls under one of four focus areas. It goes like this. The first focus area is *people*, which includes path one (the planting of new congregations) and path two (the transforming of existing congregations). The second focus area is *leaders*, which includes path three (the teaching of the United Methodist way) and path four (the strengthening of clergy and lay leadership). The third focus area is *poverty*, which includes path five (children and poverty) and path six (expanding racial/ethnic ministries). The fourth focus area is *health*, which includes only path seven (eliminating poverty by stamping out disease).[47] Again, the basic concepts are biblical and good; but for the typical church leader, the pragmatics of these four general foci with seven sub-pathways can be overwhelming, even bombastic.

45. Warren, *Purpose-Driven Church*.
46. Schnase, *Five Practices of Fruitful Congregations*.
47. Jones and Ough, *Seven Vision Pathways*.

The Need for Simplicity of Focus

Each of these models provide theoretically good and wholesome kingdom approaches. In fact, we would be challenged to find anything unbiblical in any of them. All are good. Yet, after viewing only these three (and there are many, many more!), the average United Methodist, whether a pastor or a lay person, will first become confused and perplexed, and then walk away in frustration. There are either just too many models or too many elements involved in each, or they are just way too massive and strategic for the typical person in a local church to seriously consider.[48]

In our desire for church reinvigoration, with all of the proposed purposes, practices, strategies, foci, and pathways, etc., we are actually creating a mass case of ecclesial and spiritual ADHD, and otherwise accomplishing very little. In other words, many of the church renewal models create a popular perception of overt complexity and untenability in their local application. The result is that people often become overwhelmed and give up. In contrast, Rainer and Geiger propose an idea that is pertinent to modern Methodism. We must get back to being and doing "simple church."[49] Rainer and Geiger posit that the foundational principle of being a simple church is being a church with definition; that is, being a church with both a singular clarity of purpose and singular clarity of process. They correctly state:

> Without definition, people are uncertain about *how* the church is making disciples. Without definition, people are clueless about *how* the church is designed to bring people toward spiritual maturity. Without definition, there is room for ambiguity. Most churches are ambiguous about their ministry process. . . . Church leaders must define more than the purpose (*the what*); they must also define the process (*the how*).[50]

Singular Clarity of Purpose: *The What*

In Rainer and Geiger's statement (above), *the what* is assumed: "making disciples," which means "bring[ing] people toward spiritual maturity."[51]

---

48. I can attest to this from personal experience in my own parish ministry.

49. Rainer and Geiger, *Simple Church*, 3–4.

50. Rainer and Geiger, *Simple Church*, 113–14.

51. Rainer and Geiger, *Simple Church*, 113–14.

This goal is absolutely Wesleyan. Contemporary United Methodism has done a very good job at formally defining *the what*. As such, the first line of the mission statement of The United Methodist Church is very simple and clearly delineated: "The mission of the Church is to make disciples of Jesus Christ for the transformation of the world."[52] Unfortunately, as of 2016, the second line became a bit more muddled with the addition of the extension ministries phrase: "Local churches *and extension ministries of the Church* provide the most significant arenas through which disciple-making occurs."[53] In a word (and with all due respect to the current *Discipline*)—this is not correct. We strongly assert that the proper and primary focus of United Methodism should still be to carry out the mission of making disciples within the normative bounds of *the local church*. It is the local church—and not the extension ministries—that is the key arena of discipleship development. Extension ministries are indeed significant and can serve as good contact points; they, however, should instead be understood as, and designed to be, supporters of and feeders into the ongoing Word and Sacrament ministries of the local church. Such initiatives, by their very name and nature, properly exist as effectual *extensions of the local church* and not as stand-alone entities. This concept is both very scriptural and very Wesleyan.[54] Regardless of its certainly well-meaning intention, the new wording of that second line is subtly complicating and actually diluting of the mission statement. For the sake of United Methodism, it is imperative that the mission in its entirety remains simple, streamlined, and narrowly focused.

Therefore, with this in mind, it is not in *the what* (make disciples of Jesus Christ), but rather in *the how* that the fulfillment of that mission has become frequently ambiguous, and thus rendered ineffective. In our ambiguity, we have lost our unified, church-wide alignment of common methodology. In other words, as we have become more and more vested in the concept of diversity, we have actually become a denomination functionally

52. *2016 UM Book of Discipline*, para. 120.

53. *2016 UM Book of Discipline*, para. 120 (italics mine). Note that *The Book of Discipline* from 1996 to 2012 did not have that additional phrase. (1996 was the first version of the *Book of Discipline* with the concise "make disciples" mission statement.)

54. Remember that Wesley himself spent most of his kingdom work as the leader of an extension ministry whose primary purpose was to feed and support the local parish church. In fact, prior to the Christmas Conference of 1784, Methodism, in its entirety, was essentially set up to function in a supportive role to enhance local church effectiveness.

consisting of a loose confederation of pastors, local congregations, and extension agencies that each do their own methodological thing (often under the nebulous guise of *context*). United Methodism has become not just free thinking, but free practicing as well. In so doing, we have not only ceased to be truly Wesleyan, but have also ceased to be truly Methodist. We no longer *do* what we *are*. We have forgotten the story of our beginning. Wilke very strongly speaks of our waywardness:

> Originally, we were called *Methodists* because we had a plan, an organization, a *method*. But now our methodology approaches madness, our organizational genius consumes our most sophisticated talent. Our structure has become an end in itself, not a means of saving the world. . . . [In effect] not much happens—squirrels chase other squirrels around the trees.[55]

Today, United Methodism expends much of its time and energy engaging and miring itself in busyness through such things as superficial reorganization, hollow humanitarianism, countless benevolences, sociopolitical activism, or the pursuit of this new ministry program or that, etc. As a unified church, however, we no longer authentically practice the Wesleyan concept of salvation. Borgen emphasizes that in early Methodism, Wesley's *Ordo salutis*, with Word and Sacrament at the very functional core, was the nexus of all Wesleyan ministry.[56] The point is this: As we locally, regionally, or denominationally try to embrace so many different things, we actually tend to lose sight of both our way (*the how*) and even our mission (*the what*). Again, the end result is that United Methodism is not notably making disciples and not decisively transforming the world. Yet, in echoing the optimistic tenor of Rainer and Geiger, Hamilton says, "I believe that United Methodists have an approach to the gospel that twenty-first century people will respond to and are, in fact, hungry for, if only we could be clear about what this is."[57] On this issue, Hamilton is right.

In *Jesus Pure & Simple* (2012), Cordeiro states: "Jesus did not come to complicate the gospel; He came to simplify it without compromising its purity."[58] He, in fact, sounds a lot like Wesley: "Always remember, the essence of Christian holiness is simplicity and purity; one design, one

---

55. Wilke, *And are We Yet Alive?*, 29–30.
56. Borgen, *John Wesley on the Sacraments*, 46–48.
57. Schaller, *Ice Cube is Melting*, 12.
58. Cordeiro, *Jesus*, 15.

desire; entire devotion to God."[59] Unlike with Jesus and his focused gospel of holiness, we have become our own complication. We engage in endless, disconnected "callings," and have indeed compromised the simple good news. Furthermore, in our desperation to remain a viable entity, we make incorrect assessments, focus on the wrong problems, and we apply improper solutions. For United Methodism, the necessary fix for our longtime demise is not the clever reorganization of our general agencies or our local church structures, or the finding of new ways to deal with the ordained ministry, or our restructuring into ideological jurisdictions, nor is it found in a deeper immersion into social justice and sociopolitics. The necessary fix is not in finding the next cutting-edge church growth model or popular ministry program. This is not to say that the periodic modernizing or streamlining of our administrative processes might not make us a more efficient organization. (It often can.) It is not to say that there are not societal causes which it would be prudent to support. (There often are.) It is not even to say that new church growth models and ministry programs cannot be useful. (They often can be.) However, the advocation of these causes and utilization of such programs—regardless of how honorable or functional—are still not the main solution to our missional ineffectiveness. Neither is our striving to find direct human solutions to most of the other polarizing problems that currently tear at our denomination—the "at least two or three dozen lines in the sand," as spoken of by Shaller.[60] The "lines in the sand" are indeed matters to be dealt with, but they are all symptomatic and non-foundational. McManus asks a penetrating question:

> An honest evaluation of the dramatic number of callings that the church has created would reveal that we have found extraordinary ways of describing the overwhelming amount of Christ-less living in the church. If we got the first calling right, would any of these other callings be necessary? [Remember] Jesus said, "Follow me and I will make you fishers of men."[61]

While we tinker with structural nuts and bolts and other peripheral maintenance things and otherwise engage ourselves in "the dramatic number of callings that the church has created," we remain sidetracked from seeing and dealing with the real problematic issue at hand: that is, the *spiritual poverty* that exists across the Connexion (which is manifested

---

59. Wesley, "Letters to a Member," 12:289.
60. Schaller, *Ice Cube is Melting*, 22.
61. McManus, *Unstoppable Force*, 202.

in "the overwhelming amount of Christ-less living in the church").[62] To apply Wesley's own words, we have become neglectful of "the essence of Christian holiness,"[63] and, through such a persistent remissness, we have become largely forgetful about—even blinded to—the simple and pure devotion praxis we have long disregarded.

Not faithfully following Jesus and not making disciples are both the causes and the effects of our systemic spiritual poverty. Putting band-aids on the gunshot wound is not going to do it; what we need is spiritual healing. McManus's point above should be well-taken. Consider this proposition: As Methodists, if we got back to simply following Christ through our renewed practice of the Wesleyan means of grace with Constant Word and Sacrament at the very center, would it not just be possible that God might start graciously crafting us (again) into a church of ethical disciples and synchronously causing the dramatic number of our other callings (and "lines in the sand") to become greatly reduced and perhaps even healed completely?[64] We ourselves cannot fix the situation. As much as we try to be, we are not the solution. God is. We would do well to submit ourselves to him and rely solely on his grace. Knight indicates the necessity of our own dependence upon divine grace:

> The singing of hymns, searching the scriptures, participation in the eucharist, and praying the prayers of the church all demonstrate the fundamental relatedness which is at the heart of Wesley's understanding of the experience of God. . . . Wesley uses means of grace to shift the attention to a God who is other than us, and who possesses an identity distinct from our own. Christian affections are either in relation to this God, or they are not Christian at all.[65]

Knight is making the strong point that our continuous use of the means of grace moves us from an anthropocentric to a theocentric spirituality. In using the means of grace, we practice divine dependence. We follow Jesus.

---

62. McManus, *Unstoppable Force*, 202.

63. Wesley, "Letters to a Member," 12:289.

64. For instance, see Kreider, *Communion Shapes Character*, 151–52. She asserts that through all of our "common life" encounters with God, but especially through the practice of Holy Communion, we "become a people of truly Christlike character" and "are shaped by the Spirit into a compassionate community of love."

65. Knight, *Presence of God*, 167.

Collins further adds that the grace of God we require is "not amorphous," and thus must be practiced in concrete forms, i.e., "words, signs, and actions," in order for people to be exposed to the "substance of both divine favor and empowerment."[66] Knight concurs; he says that using these concrete forms provides the interactive framework for the application of grace and our subsequent transformation:

> I have argued that the means of grace are essential to the Christian life because they give form to a distinctive, continuing relationship with God. Taken together, their pattern of mutual interaction and interdependence constitute a context within which the Christian life is formed and shaped. To participate in the means of grace is to be increasingly open to the presence and transforming power of God.[67]

The postulations of Knight and Collins are absolutely correct. Constant Word and Sacrament are essential to an ongoing relationship with God[68] because Word and Sacrament are substantive, concrete mediators of God's transforming grace to people.[69] It is here that we, in the words of Rattenbury, attend the "eucharistic meeting-place of the Savior."[70] We meet Christ and he changes us. The Wesleys founded the entire system of Methodism on this soteriologically oriented notion. Thus, contemporary Methodism is in dire need of once again becoming increasingly open to God's transforming grace and power, which is abundantly available through a continuing *practiced* communion with God. As such, Methodism would enter again into that simple and pure essence of Christian holiness.

SINGULAR CLARITY OF PROCESS: *THE HOW*

We advocate for a God-reliance solution. In the same spirit as Knight, Chan states, "The whole liturgy of Word and Sacrament is both God's word and God's action for the sake of the church."[71] Note the matter of divine dependence. The "whole liturgy" is *God's* Word and *God's* action. God has

---

66. Collins, *Theology of John Wesley*, 257.

67. Knight, *Presence of God*, 169.

68. Knight, *Presence of God*, 169.

69. Collins, *Theology of John Wesley*, 257.

70. Rattenbury, *Thoughts on Holy Communion*, 55.

71. Chan, *Liturgical Theology*, 66.

72

provided the simple church solution for the reinvigoration of United Methodism. The practice of Constant Word and Sacrament is very simple, yet supernaturally powerful. It is the foundational process for making people into disciples of Jesus Christ. Constant Word and Sacrament praxis is the primary conduit by which God does his greatest transformative and empowering work in and through us as the church. Schillebeeckx speaks of the effect of sacramental communion with God, which he defines as "theologal activity":

> Theologal activity in grace, a life lived for God, is expressed in moral behavior. . . . Hence, moral virtue comes to depend upon personal communion with God; it becomes the embodiment of our divine communion on every plane of human living, and so serves and promotes the life of grace. Therefore the sacramental encounter with Christ affects the whole of the Christian moral life. Through the God-centred grace which they give, and through our fidelity to this grace, the Sacraments heal the "wounds of nature" and build up in us the "new man" in the image of Christ. . . . [Thus] The fruitfulness of a Sacrament in grace, then, includes all the richness of Christian life in communion with the Church, the visible sign of grace in which the fullness of Christ is present. The Church, the *pleroma* [fullness] of Christ, fills us with the fullness of him who is filled with the fullness of God. And this is man's encounter with God in full mutual availability.[72]

Schillebeeckx holds that as we regularly submit ourselves to encounter Christ, we become exposed to the healing and edifying power of God. God transforms our soul, our shattered divine image, and our entire life.[73] Since "sacramental grace is sanctifying grace itself,"[74] we are enabled to demonstrate our deep commitment to Christ in a personal relationship and engage in the efficacy of his gospel through our sustained submission to the whole liturgy of Word and Sacrament.

Through such submission, God will save us and change us to save and change the world. God has given Word and Sacrament for the sake of the church.[75] God has given the church for the sake of the world. Conversely, the negation of Constant Word and Sacrament praxis in our local congregations means the depletion of our ethical discipleship development and

---

72. Schillebeeckx, *Christ the Sacrament*, 183–84.

73. Schillebeeckx, *Christ the Sacrament*, 183–84.

74. Schillebeeckx, *Christ the Sacrament*, 182.

75. Chan, *Liturgical Theology*, 66.

the correspondent omission of our making of other disciples. When we are not disciples and do not make other disciples, we do not transform the world. When we do not make disciples and transform the world, we die. To use Vahanian's imagery, we are functioning as if God is dead.[76]

The Need for Restoration of Holiness of Heart

Just as in Wesley's day with the Church of England, the problem is not primarily in our basic ecclesial structure or even in our variant beliefs[77]; it is our heart; or, put specifically in Wesleyan terms, it is our lack of holiness of heart. We have grown away from the cornerstone of Christ by neglecting his preeminent means of grace. Instead, we have fallen prey to what Cordeiro calls, "the lure of a complicated devotion."[78] With the very best of intentions, we have become so devoted to healing so many variant evils and perceived injustices in the world, and so devoted to promoting so many different blessings in the world, that we have actually fallen away in our communal devotion to the very One who is the Source of all real healing and all that is truly blessed and good. In our mere human efforts to do no evil and to do only good, we have failed to be faithful in our practice of the preeminent ordinances of God: Constant Word and Sacrament. We have become so focused on our works of mercy (attempting to do the compassionate and just tasks of disciples) that we have woefully neglected our works of piety (actually becoming holy and empowered disciples). In so doing, even our well-intentioned attempts at works of mercy are merely broken and depraved futilities of social justice that are devoid of God's power. Sadly, we have become a brand of the very people against whom Paul cautioned: those who are trying to practice "the form of religion but denying the power of it" (2 Tim 3:5). This is why we are dying.

---

76. See Vahanian, *Death of God.*

77. We refer to *opinions* here, not *essentials.* Wesley made clear distinction between the two (see Borgen, *John Wesley on the Sacraments,* 38–43). Of course, we also aver that a growing holiness of heart will also begin to alleviate many deviations of belief. As we grow closer to Christ (who is the Truth), we become more aware and accepting of that which is true. God does this through Constant Word and Sacrament. God transforms minds, hearts, and lives.

78. Cordeiro, *Jesus,* 14. Remember, Wesley advocates for a simple and focused devotion (Wesley, "Letters to a Member," 12:289). His goal was always to remain "on a single eye" (Wesley, "On a Single Eye," 4:120–30).

Wesley would certainly disavow such a "dead sect" misappropriation of the Christian faith.[79] In his work, *A Plain Account of Christian Perfection* (1777), Wesley says:

> I saw it would not profit me to give my entire life to God (assuming it is possible to do so, and go no further) unless I give God my heart. I saw the need for "simplicity of intention, and purity of affection."[80]

Eschewing Wesley's wisdom, we have chosen the less profitable form of the faith and largely disregarded what Harper calls, "the first mark of discipleship." He asserts:

> The first mark of discipleship isn't a call to increase our love but to receive God's love. The ability to love God [and others] comes from God! This is no self-help effort, no intensification of our devotion through a spiritual version of trying harder. The call to love God is a call extended by none other than God. . . . this isn't a natural love; it is supernatural. . . . Wesley's call to love is one to which we respond, "I can't do this on my own!" This is right where he wanted the people called Methodist to be: people who renounce all attempts to love from the source of self, and who now receive the invitation to love from the source of grace. . . . Wesley is leading us to embrace the disposition of our hearts, from which everything else flows.[81]

Holiness of heart is a necessary prerequisite for holiness of life. Our works of piety empower our works of mercy.[82] Thus, following this thought of Harper (and Wesley), we seem to have placed the proverbial cart before the horse. We have been trying to love from the source of self and not from the source of grace.

In effect, United Methodism has created and implemented a bastard form of Wesley's *Three General Rules* (1739) by trying to self-accomplish

---

79. Wesley, "Thoughts Upon Methodism," 9:527. In this short essay (1786), Wesley began with these prophetic words: "I am not afraid that the people called Methodists should ever cease to exist either in Europe or America. But I am afraid lest they should only exist as a dead sect, having the form of religion without the power. And this undoubtedly will be the case unless they hold fast both the doctrine, spirit, and discipline with which they first set out."

80. Wesley, *Plain Account of Christian Perfection*, 5. Also, see Wesley, "On a Single Eye," 4:120–30.

81. Harper, *Five Marks of a Methodist*, 7–9.

82. For further, see Job, *Wesleyan Spiritual Reader*, 99–100.

the first two without utilizing the fullness of the third.[83] Such a skewed methodology will not accomplish the work of the church and advance the kingdom of God. As Job asserts in his *Three Simple Rules* (2007)—a contemporary adaptation and commentary of Wesley's *Three General Rules*—the third rule (which he describes as "Stay[ing] in love with God"[84]) is the efficacious key to the success of the others:

> Wesley saw these disciplines [the ordinances of God with Word and Sacrament worship being preeminent] as central to any life of faithfulness to God in Christ. He saw that the consistent practice of these spiritual disciplines kept those who sought to follow Christ in touch with the presence and power of Christ so they could fulfill their desire to live as faithful disciples.[85]

By rejecting Wesley's discipleship methodology and thus not placing the practice of Word and Sacrament worship at the very front and center of our ecclesial lives, we have effectually fallen out of love with God and have spurned "the presence and power of Christ." The result is that we, as a whole, despite our good intentions, are *not able* to live as faithful disciples. We lack the power to do so, and thus have largely become that dead sect so feared by Wesley. Chilcote drives home the point:

> Wesley realized that true evangelism (God's Word proclaimed) could only be grounded in worship, and the center of Christian worship was the meeting place of pulpit and table. The full, rich and joyous eucharistic life of early Methodists is one of the best-kept secrets of the tradition. It is a tragedy today that so few of Wesley's heirs know about this side of the revival.[86]

It is indeed tragic because it is from Constant Word and Sacrament worship praxis that all other disciplines, means of grace, and ministries radiate. The demise of our numbers and impact are just outward signs of our flagging zeal for God and our corresponding neglect of functional communion with God. After all, as Harper asserts, it is in "the disposition of

---

83. Remember, the *Three General Rules* of the United Societies are: [1] Do no harm; [2] Do only good; and [3] Attend upon all the ordinances of God (See 2016 *UM Book of Discipline*, Para. 104, 78–80).

84. Job, *Three Simple Rules*, 53.

85. Job, *Three Simple Rules*, 53–54.

86. Chilcote, *Recapturing the Wesleys' Vision*, 84.

our hearts [holiness of heart], from which everything else flows."[87] Borgen provides this honest assessment:

> On the background of such a situation, which, of course, will admit of exceptions, the need for a recovery of Wesley's basic emphases is urgently needed. The basic lack of God-given spiritual power will demand that the means of grace again be given, not reverence, but a dynamic function in the common, as well as in the private, life. Only through a disciplined use of these means, springing out of hearts longing to see their people and their church arise with new spiritual vigor, can the great task of renewal be made possible.[88]

We lack "spiritual vigor" because we lack "God-given spiritual power." We lack divine spiritual power because we have become neglectful of the Wesleyan nexus of grace. Our divine connection has been severed. We have unwittingly become a church predicated on anthropocentric endeavor.[89] We have little true holiness of life (loving mission with God) because we have little true holiness of heart (loving communion with God).

In concurrence with the spirit of Job, Chilcote, and Borgen, it is important that we immediately engage in the widespread reimplementation of the classic Wesleyan praxis of Constant Word and Sacrament. We should begin by exposing our current constituency to a steady weekly diet of Word and Sacrament which will provide for God to supernaturally reinvigorate our denomination. While we are co-participants, it will be God—not us—who will do the reinvigoration. He will take it upon himself to light the spiritual fire (Heb 12:28–29; cf. Matt 3:12). Our portion is, as Wilke says, to simply burn for Christ.[90] We burn and keep the fires burning by relentlessly practicing Constant Word and Sacrament.

Since, as Payne said, "God wants the church to make disciples,"[91] then, applying Chan's thought, Word and Sacrament praxis for "the sake of the church" implies the central place that such sustained "whole liturgy" has in the disciple-making process.[92] It is actually God who supernaturally makes disciples (i.e., it is God's Word, God's action) in and through his

---

87. Harper, *Five Marks of a Methodist*, 9.

88. Borgen, *John Wesley on the Sacraments*, 281.

89. Borgen, *John Wesley on the Sacraments*, 282.

90. Wilke, *And are We Yet Alive?*, 107–24.

91. Payne, *American Methodism*, ix; also, see the Great Commission statements of Matthew 28:18–20; Mark 16:15–18; Luke 24:45–49, and Acts 1:8.

92. Chan, *Liturgical Theology*, 66.

co-participating church (i.e., by submission to right liturgical practice; cf. Heb 12:28). Therefore, Chan is asserting that the power of God is available to the church for the purpose of discipleship through his primary chosen means of Constant Word and Sacrament worship praxis. Through Word and Sacrament, the people encounter God and experience anew the gift of his transforming gospel. Following Chan, we contend that the whole re-demptive power of God is available to the people of God through the whole liturgy (Word *and* Sacrament) of God.

Chappell, like Chan, speaks of what God brings to worship. Citing Psalm 16:11 and 144:15, he avers that God brings himself glory and brings us his goodness.[93] Both of these are the goals of worship:

> By his presence in our lives God intends to bring himself glory *and* to bring us his goodness (Pss 16:11; 144:15). The gospel is God's means of conquering the effects of sin for precisely these purposes. Through our apprehension and appropriation of the gospel, God receives glory and we partake of his goodness. Worship that represents [re-presents] the gospel must have these same goals. Worship is not only for God's glory, and it is not only for our good. In order for the gospel to be good news for God's people it must have both goals, and worship that is reflective of the gospel must also have both goals.[94]

By his personal presence, God is at work giving his goodness and vir-tue to his people through Christ-centered sacramental worship. In this, we become perfected and God receives glory. Chappell emphasizes the inten-sive and extensive implications of such sacramentality:

---

93. This, of course, fits the reality of James 1:16–18: "Do not be deceived, my beloved brethren. Every good endowment and every perfect gift is from above, coming down from the Father of lights with whom there is no variation or shadow due to change. Of his own will he brought us forth by the word of truth that we should be a kind of first fruits of his creatures." Please do not miss that, within the purview of God, his *good* and his *perfect* are synonymous (cf. Mark 10:18 and Luke 18:19; see also, Wesley, "God's Approbation of His Works," 2:387–99). Thus, the ultimate soteriological purpose of the work of God is the restoration of his good and perfect original creation (Gen 1:31), which became marred and distorted at the Adamic fall (Gen 3; see also, Wesley, "General Deliverance," 2:437–50; cf. Stallings, *Genesis Column*, esp. 7–32). While God is restoring the entire created order (think cosmic *missio Dei*), he is preeminently bringing glory to himself by invoking such a good/perfect transformation in us—the fallen crown of his creation—through our co-participation with him in sacramental worship praxis.

94. Chappell, *Christ-Centered Worship*, 119.

God uses our worship to strengthen us as well as to glorify himself. We need not exempt concern for ministering to one another from our worship priorities. The gospel pattern of biblical worship indicates that it is meant to minister God's goodness as well as to proclaim his glory to his people. In our worship we do not merely "point back" to God's mighty acts, but we also "make present" his saving reality. The gospel represented in the structures of our worship pictures the story of redemption while also enabling us to re-enter that narrative and to live its truths with the Savior they make present to each new generation's experience.[95]

The practice of Constant Word and Sacrament enables us to actively engage in a personal and empowering relationship with God by our remaining continuously present in the redemptive and transforming reality of the Risen Christ. This is the simple solution to our current stagnation. Those who are immersed in complicated devotion might revile at the utter simplicity of this notion; but nonetheless, the key to curing the woes of the United Methodist Church is, first and foremost, to completely build everything around Christ-centered sacramental worship in the local church. Chilcote gently admonishes us:

> We need a balanced diet of proclamation and participation, sermon and Sacrament, pulpit and table. Most Methodists do not realize that the Wesleyan revival was both evangelical (a rediscovery of the importance of the Word) and eucharistic (a rediscovery of the Sacrament of Holy Communion). The Wesleys and the early Methodists held both together, firmly convinced that both were necessary for proper guidance in the Christian faith and walk. sacramental grace and evangelical experience were viewed as necessary counterparts of a balanced Christian life. The enthusiasm for the Sacrament of the Lord's Supper among the early Methodists was the result of zeal kindled in the hearts of the people by the flaming message of God's love. And so the combination of the pulpit and the table was like a two-edged sword; the conjunction was a potent agent in the spread of the revival.[96]

It is time for United Methodism to recover the practical and proven wisdom of the Wesleys and again draw this two-edged sword—the *potent agent* of revival.

---

95. Chappell, *Christ-Centered Worship*, 119–20.

96. Chilcote, *Recapturing the Wesleys' Vision*, 80–81.

The Contemporary Application

Our divine worship is the key to our revitalization. Our primary service of divine worship is the launching pad for our revival. Constant Word and Sacrament praxis in our service of worship is the God-chosen tool for the recovery and ongoing sustenance of Methodist spiritual and missional power. There are three simple steps to our single-focus revitalization: [1] retrain our sacramental understanding; [2] implement a Wesleyan-Biblical delivery system; and [3] unleash the work of God.

The Simple Method of Single-focus Revitalization

Step One: Retrain Our sacramental Understanding

United Methodism must be retrained so as to recover the fullness of sacramental Christianity. This training must begin with the pastoral leadership and then move outward. The clergy must become both convinced and convicted of the sacramental reality of God. In *A Better Way* (2002), Horton stresses that "the action really is [in] the genuine 'signs and wonders' ministry that God performs each week when the word is rightly preached and the Sacraments are rightly administered."[97] This is the reality that must be fully recovered and embraced by the clergy first, and then passed on to the laity.

Specifically, we must come to understand that when the Bible-as-Scripture is not maximally proclaimed, that is, publicly read as a proclamation of God's Word as well as passionately preached as a proclamation of God's Word (and also taught outside of worship in the same spirit),[98] there remains an underlying belief in the insignificance of scriptural truth and efficacy. Likewise, we must understand that when the Holy Sacrament is not administered at least every Sunday (and other times during the week, if at all possible), there remains an underlying belief that Constant Communion

---

97. Horton, *Better Way*, 161.

98. Willimon and Wilson, *Rekindling the Flame*, 80–87. They observe: "Many people in the contemporary church, including many committed Christians, do not have an adequate understanding of their faith. Biblical illiteracy, of the sort that John Wesley would have deplored, is rampant. This occurs despite the fact that the Bible is central to United Methodism's understanding of the faith. This lack of understanding comes at a time when the level of formal education of United Methodist clergy and of most of the laity has never been higher" (81).

is really not effectual and therefore just not necessary.[99] Both of these realities betray a widespread deficiency of understanding within the church, among both the clergy and the laity, as to the divine nourishment and power inherently provided through Word and Sacrament praxis. Bouyer argues that worship without the centrality of *both* Word and Sacrament is an aimless endeavor that "means no more than worship without formula and rites."[100] Such insufficient worship, asserts Webber and others, reveals a significant break with the practices of the Wesleyan tradition and the biblical faith (see Acts 2:42, 46).[101]

Much of our worship today is like this. It invokes only the natural capacity of depraved human action and not the transforming power of the Living God.[102] We Methodists must come to an awareness of this and be led to see the need for correction. In many contemporary circles, in fact, the sermon has become merely a human-centered self-help device while Communion is treated as an occasional take-it-or-leave-it ritual, fraught only with some sort of weak Zwinglian symbolism. This hollow human-centeredness is unfortunate, for as Webber states:

> According to Scripture, the human race is spiritually lost and in need of direction. Yet, out of his love for us, God provides signs to give us a sure sense of direction. But unlike the directional highway signs with which we are so familiar, God's signs are not passive. Rather, in and through them, God acts toward us and communicates his love and grace to us, so that we are not left to uncertainty, despair, and frustration. Biblical history is rich with signs pointing to God's purposes. But today, I believe, it is in worship that God gives us signs of his grace. *In worship God speaks and acts.*[103]

We must be retrained to understand that non-sacramental worship is devoid of this. It is a weak and impoverished worship with little or no efficacy. Thus, Webber becomes even more explicit:

> And throughout church history, God's initiative in grace has always been accomplished by tangible and concrete signs. For

99. Bouyer, *Word, Church and Sacraments*, 70–72.

100. Bouyer, *Word, Church and Sacraments*, 72.

101. Webber, *Worship Old & New*, 95–106; Wesley, "Duty of Constant Communion," 3:428–39; Westerfield-Tucker, *American Methodist Worship*, 118–19.

102. Horton, *Better Way*, 10–17.

103. Webber, *Worship is a Verb*, 65–66 (italics his).

example, in worship I experience God's presence and action toward me through the sign of the Bible and through the signs of bread and wine, the Holy Communion. In turn, I respond to God through these signs. This means that in worship there is a descending line established by God and an ascending line represented by my faith. And the intersecting point of these lines is the visible and tangible sign of God's grace: the Bible together with the bread and the wine.[104]

As Webber indicates, Word and Sacrament are interconnected divine/human lifelines. In such worship, the lives of God and humanity meet. It is there that God mediates grace in the most profound way.[105] At the creation, the Word of God (Greek *logos*) spoke and acted for our original life to come into being (John 1:1–3). In Word and Sacrament, as a continual reapplication of Christ's once-and-for-all atonement, the same Word of God speaks and acts for our original life to be remade anew (cf. John 1:12–14, 16). It is no wonder that when these liturgical lifelines (Word *and* Sacrament) between God and people are either neglected in functional practice, or relegated to being something less than conveyances of grace, that the spiritual formation of the church's constituency and its transformational power in the world experiences great weakness and loss. White calls such a result "an inevitable development."[106]

In *Unchristian* (2007), Kinnaman and Lyons go so far as to assert that large segments of the contemporary church do not display lives that are visibly transformed by Christ.[107] It surely stands to reason that the church cannot be very transforming if it is not itself transformed. As either one of these essentials, Word or Sacrament, becomes neglected, the body of Christ willfully chooses to be at least partially cut off from God, who is the supernatural source of life and power. In doing so, the body chooses to become and remain spiritually feeble, only receiving half or less of what it needs for abundance and growth into Christlikeness. Sadly, much of United Methodism has become such a self-starving body. Yet, that is not the Wesleyan way.

A renewal of supernatural power in the church is urgently needed. Cherry stresses her belief that this will only happen with a full recovery

---

104. Webber, *Worship is a Verb*, 66–67.

105. Collins, *Theology of John Wesley*, 257.

106. White, *Sacraments in Protestant Practice*, 23.

107. Kinnaman and Lyons, *Unchristian*, 46–48.

of historic Christian worship practices, inclusive of a Christocentric sacramental faith.[108] She says:

> The cornerstone of Christian worship is Jesus Christ. This truth alone determines the authenticity of Christian worship. . . . You will recall that the purpose of any cornerstone, architecturally speaking, is to serve as the foundational piece from which the structure is measured to be true. Once the cornerstone is in place, all else flows from there. Laying the cornerstone must be a priority, then, for if it is slighted, the entire structure is compromised.[109]

Webber further clarifies Cherry's "Jesus is the worship cornerstone" concept:

> Now, because God has appeared in the flesh in Jesus, new signs are established to communicate his presence. The most important signs of God's grace in Jesus Christ are the Bible and the Sacrament of bread and wine.[110]

Therefore, following Cherry and Webber, Jesus is the cornerstone of worship because he is most powerfully present and active in worship through Word and Sacrament praxis. This is the essence of historic Christian worship.[111] In light of this, as United Methodism has moved increasingly away from historic sacramental worship, the entire denominational edifice has gradually become compromised from the worship ground up. Schnase presents a reparative solution:

> Vibrant, fruitful, growing churches offer passionate worship that connects people to God and one another. People gather consciously as the Body of Christ with eagerness and expectancy; encounter Christ through singing, prayer, Scripture, preaching and Holy Communion, and respond by allowing God's Spirit to shape their lives. Lives shaped by God's Spirit become the nucleus for congregations with extraordinary warmth, graciousness, and belonging. People are searching for worship that is authentic, alive, creative, and comprehensible, where they experience the life-changing presence of God in the presence of others.[112]

---

108. Cherry, *Worship Architect*, 19–32.
109. Cherry, *Worship Architect*, 21.
110. Webber, *Worship is a Verb*, 69.
111. Senn, *Stewardship of the Mysteries*, 5.
112. Schnase, *Five Practices of Fruitful Congregations*, 33.

In other words, in order to fully receive much-needed life renewal in Christ, United Methodists must *get back to the [sacramental worship] spout where the glory comes out.*[113] Our sacramental re-education—clergy first, and then laity—is essential. That is the Wesleyan way.

STEP TWO: IMPLEMENT A WESLEYAN-BIBLICAL DELIVERY SYSTEM

This is where clergy need to firmly take the reins of leadership. Divine worship is crucial and indispensable to the transformational Christian life. This is true both individually and congregationally. As Stetzer and Rainer remind us: "Worship is perhaps the most important action of the human experience. . . .Transformational churches place worship at the center point."[114] The rampant implementation of Constant Word and Sacrament worship through a practical and effective Wesleyan-biblical delivery system is highly recommended. It is, in fact, imperative. In *Worship in the Shape of Scripture* (2001), Mitman suggests that this delivery system, of course, should be the classic fourfold order of Sunday worship: the Gathering, the Word, the Table, and the Sending.[115] He calls this format the "organic liturgy" because it is shaped by the message of Scripture and the dialogical interaction between God and his church.[116] Mitman says:

> The interconnectedness associated with an organic approach to liturgy is fundamentally a reflection of the very nature of the church itself, in New Testament images, as the *body* of Christ with Christ at the center and all the members working in harmony. The

113. Early Methodists frequently used variations of this *spout* image to refer to sacramental communion with God and to the abundant grace that they knew flowed from it. The implication was that one needs to go to ("get under") the spout in order to drink from the transformative living water. It was typically associated with the ordinary means of grace, but especially Holy Communion. (Remember, Wesley used the living water image when he referred to the Lord's Supper as "the grand channel," i.e., the gushing fountain, the flowing river, etc.) As Harper says, "Some of our predecessors had a phrase for it: 'You have to be at the spout where the glory comes out.' They meant that if we are actually going to drink of the Water of Life, we have to be at the places where it flows" (Harper, *Prayer & Devotional Life*, 42).

114. Stetzer and Rainer, *Transformational Church*, 149.

115. Mitman, *Worship in the Shape*, 35; Cherry, *Worship Architect*, 48–49; see also, *UM Book of Worship* (1992), 13–15. Remember, Cherry says that "the [four-fold] order is the gospel" (49).

116. Mitman, *Worship in the Shape*, 32–34.

whole of worship is a total event of integrally related and mutually dependent acts through which the Word of God seeks embodiment in the community of faith.[117]

If we, following the teaching of Webber, understand that the Scriptures do indeed reveal a great, overarching metanarrative that encompasses God's sacramental interaction throughout all of reality from original creation through this present age and onto the eschatological consummation and the New Creation, then it seems that the church would do well to practice worship in a way that easily communicates and demonstrates this truth.[118] Webber posits that biblical "worship . . . does God's story."[119] As such, in the words of Mitman, "through the whole of worship . . . the Word of God seeks embodiment in the community of faith."[120] This is worship that is divinely transforming of the worshipper. The active presence of the living Word of God (Greek *logos*) in the sustained practices of Word (Word-in-text) and Sacrament (Word-at-table) liturgy changes people and causes them to become more like Christ. (The expression of *logos* through proclamative interaction combined with the expression of *logos* through eucharistic interaction is what brings about maximal divine transformation.) Therefore, in the understanding of Webber, the formative and transformative gospel is in the practiced liturgy.[121] It follows then, as Smith stresses, that God enables the liturgical practices themselves to teach, inculcate, and form the truth of the gospel into the minds and hearts of people.[122] Using Mitman's image above, the Word of God becomes *embodied* in people through sacramental praxis. Horton adds:

> The important thing to see in all this is that worship is the divine drama. In it, the drama of redemption that unfolds in biblical history now unfolds as a play before us in a particular place and our own time. In it, we join Abraham and Sarah at the table with their greater Son through whom all the nations of the earth are blessed. With circumcised hearts, we join the cloud of witnesses who longed for Jesus' coming and the sending of his Spirit. Not just once but week after week, year after year, decade after decade,

117. Mitman, *Worship in the Shape*, 33 (italics his).

118. Webber, *Ancient-Future Worship*, 21–40.

119. Webber, *Ancient-Future Worship*, 21.

120. Mitman, *Worship in the Shape*, 33.

121. Webber, *Liturgical Evangelism*, 1–14.

122. Smith, *Desiring the Kingdom*, 148–51.

we are being reshaped by his counter-drama, as the plot of "this passing evil age" yields to "the age to come."[123]

Similarly, Pfatteicher declares, "So our relationship to the liturgy, to ourselves, and to the world is deepened and renewed; and worship, specifically the Holy Communion, becomes the center and source of our renewal, for in worship we meet God, who makes all things new."[124] Therefore, in view of this, and according to both Webber and Mitman, Christian worship should always be shaped by God's truthful story of the world and universe.[125] After all, as the church fulfills both its ontological purpose to glorify God and to receive his self-giving in worship, and its missional purpose to make disciples of Jesus Christ, the church is simultaneously co-participating in the cosmic *missio Dei* and advancing the kingdom of God (2 Cor 5:16–21). In Webber's observations, this means that the most powerful worship is that which constantly seeks to re-present the gospel by enacting the dynamic sacramental relationship that the Lord has with all creation and that believers have (and always have had) with the living God.[126] This is the sacramental inference of Mitman when he states, "The Word spoken will become the Word enacted" (cf. Isa 55:11).[127]

In this same vein, Cherry points out that the classic fourfold order of worship, emphasizing and demonstrating a biblical "conversational" pattern of divine revelation and human response, most plausibly accomplishes and gives concrete expression to this reality.[128] This is because God himself is personally encountered, both verbally and nonverbally, in the Word and Sacrament liturgy.[129] As Mitman explains:

> Liturgy is the totality of what happens verbally and nonverbally when the people of God find themselves in dialogue with the triune God who initiates the conversation and seeks to become enfleshed in the event of Word and Sacrament.[130]

---

123. Horton, *Better Way*, 161.

124. Pfatteicher, *Liturgical Spirituality*, 251.

125. Webber, *Ancient-Future Worship*, 23; Mitman, *Worship in the Shape*, 34–43.

126. Webber, *Worship Old & New*, 73–82.

127. Mitman, *Worship in the Shape*, 44.

128. Cherry, *Worship Architect*, 46–47.

129. Cf. Tyson, *Way of the Wesleys*, 144.

130. Mitman, *Worship in the Shape*, 33.

Essentially, the entire fourfold worship liturgy becomes one grand sacramental—even incarnational—movement. Through sacramental worship, the "people of God find themselves in dialogue with the triune God" because he becomes "enfleshed in the event."[131] In light of the dominant theological assertion that Word and Sacrament should be at the very heart and life of every local congregation, and as such are thus indispensable to every primary worship service, the fourfold schematic delivers flawlessly.[132]

For United Methodists, such a practice of Christian worship should be considered as completely non-negotiable. UM pastors should take heed. Since Word-Sacrament is the primary appointed *spout where God's glory comes out*, all United Methodists should be given the opportunity to drink from it as much and as often as possible. This can and should begin now.

Step Three: Unleash the Work of God

Word and Sacrament worship is an expectant worship. It is supernatural in its origin, expression, and destination. God is personally present and active.[133] It is worship that expects and anticipates God to do extraordinary things because, as Knight says:

> [H]e is present in both ordinary and extraordinary ways, at the Lord's table as well as in awakening phenomena like falling to the ground, in Scripture and sermon, as much as in dreams and visions . . . through the power of the Holy Spirit, God can and does transform lives, renew churches, and reform society, all in ways that more faithfully mirror the life of the coming kingdom.[134]

This expectancy is what Knight calls the Wesleyan "optimism of grace."[135] We enter into sacramental worship with this optimism of grace. We experience the proclamation of the sacramental Word with this optimism of grace. We come to the sacramental Table with this optimism of grace. We are then sent forth into the sacramental world with this same optimism of grace.

---

131. Mitman, *Worship in the Shape*, 33.

132. Chan, *Liturgical Theology*, 62–70.

133. Hickman, *Worshipping With United Methodists*, 24.

134. Knight, *Anticipating Heaven Below*, 246–47.

135. Knight, *Anticipating Heaven Below*, xi–247.

In consonance with Knight, Stookey reiterates this Wesleyan eucharistic expectancy:

> The Eucharist is the feast of the whole church as it participates in and yet awaits the perfect reign of God. And what we expect to become, we seek to be now. . . . [and] . . . Those who glimpse the kingdom in the kingdom meal called the Eucharist thereafter strive to do already on earth what they have envisioned to be done in heaven.[136]

Stookey is emphasizing that in sacramental worship, God works toward both our *becoming* and our *doing*. Through it, we ourselves become more holy and then we are driven to do works of holiness. Thus, in true Word and Sacrament worship, filled with the certainty of divine optimism, we know that we will encounter God; we know that we will be transformed by God; and we know that we will be empowered by God to engage in the great work of God.

Word and Sacrament worship is biblical worship because the biblical God is supremely active, redemptive, and transformative in such worship. Word and Sacrament worship is also biblical worship because in it and through it God gives grace and moves people further along the way of salvation. Webber declares:

> Worship is all about how God, with his own two hands—the incarnate Word and the Holy Spirit—has rescued the world. The biblical God is an active God—he creates, becomes active in the world to rescue his creation from sin and death, and restores the world to paradise and beyond in the new heavens and new earth.[137]

He also adds:

> Not only does worship point to the culmination of all history in the new heavens and new earth, but it also shapes the ethical behavior of God's people to reflect kingdom ethics here on earth. Consequently, the ethical life of the church is an eschatological witness to the world of how people should be living and how the world will be under the reign of God.[138]

Thus, in Word and Sacrament worship, God calls us; God speaks to us; God gives to us; God sends us. As we encounter God, we are changed

136. Stookey, *Eucharist*, 26.

137. Webber, *Ancient-Future Worship*, 66.

138. Webber, *Ancient-Future Worship*, 66.

and we are compelled to mission. This is the great and supernatural work of God that will transpire through his faithful people until the end of this present age and the advent of the New Kingdom.[139]

Significantly, Senn invokes an additional dimension. He adds that worship which fully utilizes the means of grace is also a matter of good stewardship.[140] After all, Paul wrote in 1 Corinthians 4:1, "This is how one should regard us, as servants of Christ and stewards of the mysteries of God." Since God's Word and God's Sacrament are his mysterious and efficacious gifts to his church, we would do well to constantly utilize both of them in our worship as "sign-acts of the proclamation of the saving cross of Christ."[141] In light of this, our contrary lack of constant usage within Methodism of these "sign-acts" can be understood as a lack of effective stewardship which diminishes our participation in the work of God.

According to Cherry, biblical worship, i.e., worship which "flows from the person and work of God" via Word and Sacrament, is the key to the recovery of new life for the church.[142] Such new life worship is effectually the worship of Easter people, which is the true identity of all of us who are in Christ. Through Constant Word and Sacrament, we—who are already raised with Christ—continually encounter the Risen Christ, who gives us renewed faith and power and an ongoing message of new life for the world.[143] It is the Risen Christ who is the *actual Declarer* of the Word proclaimed; it is the Risen Christ who is the *actual Host* of the Table administered. And it is precisely here that we can light the flame of a new and life-changing Methodist revival not unlike that spawned by Wesley.

Some years ago, in their book *Rekindling the Flame* (1987), Willimon and Wilson sounded the alarm. They recommended that in order to stimulate revitalization, the United Methodist Church would need to "Give priority to Sunday Morning."[144] Of course, worship renewal was in mind. If the church of Jesus Christ, including United Methodism, is, as Chan asserts, most powerfully expressed as a community of people assembled together and actively engaged in the worship of the Triune God,[145] then this rec-

139. Pfatteicher, *Liturgical Spirituality*, 251–53; Senn, *Stewardship of the Mysteries*, 8.

140. Senn, *Stewardship of the Mysteries*, 2–3.

141. Senn, *Stewardship of the Mysteries*, 3.

142. Cherry, *Worship Architect*, 3–5.

143. Hickman, *Worshipping With United Methodists*, 24.

144. Willimon and Wilson, *Rekindling the Flame*, 111–20.

145. Chan, *Liturgical Theology*, 42–48.

ommendation makes perfect sense. This is especially true for Methodism since the Methodist-Evangelical Revival was very much a liturgical revival focused on the practice of Word and Sacrament.[146]

As Jennings strongly documents in his book, *The Supernatural Occurrences of John Wesley* (2012), the overtly supernatural work of God was once very prominent in Methodism.[147] It was especially prominent at the celebration of Word and Sacrament. In fact, as Ruth points out in *A Little Heaven Below* (2000), the term "work of God" was a quite common idiom used by the early Methodists to describe occurrences in their worship associated with God's sacramental presence and power.[148] Regarding God's presence:

> One recurring aspect in American Methodists' accounts of administration of the Lord's Supper is a strong affirmation of God's presence. Rather than saying early Methodists had a "high" *doctrine* of sacramental presence, it is more accurate to say they had a "high" *sense* of it because the categories that they normally used to describe divine presence were drawn from the intensely affective nature of their piety. . . . "the presents [sic] of the Lord was powerfully felt" . . . "the Lord met with us in Maraculous [sic] Manner, a time of refreshment from his presence" . . . Such encounter with the presence of God in the Sacrament could be understood as an experience that transposed the Methodist fellowship: "our good God was pleased to meet us at his table." At times the intense sensibility of God's presence led Methodists to experience what they called "raptures" or "ecstacies" of joy in the Sacrament.[149]

The visibly manifested presence of God in the sacramental worship of early Methodism also meant that the power of God was also present, active, and available. Regarding also God's power:

> Although the circumstances and the people themselves might have been humble, Methodist affirmation that God was present in their Sacrament was often connected with a notion of God's power. If God was present, then God was present in power. . . .

146. Khoo, *Wesleyan Eucharistic Spirituality*, 107; Willimon and Wilson, *Rekindling the Flame*, 113; cf. Chilcote, *Recapturing the Wesleys' Vision*, 84–85; also, Chilcote, "Fullness of Learning," 72. Chilcote avers that the "Wesleyan tradition—[is] a heritage defined in large measure by its eucharistic spirituality."

147. Jennings, *Supernatural Occurrences of John Wesley*, 2–3.

148. Ruth, *Little Heaven Below*, 139, 141.

149. Ruth, *Little Heaven Below*, 138 (italics his).

[Many] accounts make God's presence synonymous with God's power by noting that during the Sacrament, "the power came down." Sometimes the presence of God in power and the resultant outbreak of the "work of God" [even] forced an interruption in distribution of the bread and wine. . . . [Documented attestations include:] "the work of sanctification amongst the believers broke out at the Lord's Table; and the spirit of the Lord went through the assembly like a mighty rushing wind" [and] When "the Lord made bare his arm" at another Lord's Supper "sinners were convicted, backsliders were reclaimed, mourners were converted, and many brought to struggle for full redemption in the blood of Jesus."[150]

Ruth's descriptions show an experiential dimension to EAM sacramentalism that seems to be missing in much of our worship and missional life today. Where is the regular "outbreak of the 'work of God'" in our United Methodist worship? Moreover, where is that same regular outbreak in our United Methodist missional life? It does not seem to be presently active in its fullness. There is, however, no reason whatsoever to believe that this same "work of God," with the Lord himself in full presence and power, cannot again become fully active in contemporary United Methodism. We must recover and reactivate the primary medium of God's working grace. Following Senn, we require a renewed good stewardship of Word and Sacrament praxis.

In his book, *The Supernatural Thread in Methodism* (2013), Billman, in concurrence with Cherry, Willimon, and Ruth, stresses that Methodism needs "the work of God" to again be manifestly present in our services of worship.[151] A recovery of Constant Word and Sacrament will again open the floodgates of the life and power of God, i.e., the *work of God*, into United Methodism. As such, we may again become, as Ruth asserts, "singularly owned of God."[152] As was the case among the early Methodists, God will maximally drive people into discipleship and mission through the preaching and teaching of his Holy Word combined with the regular life-giving encounters with him through his Holy Sacrament. Through these sustained worship practices, God will again cause Methodists to have and develop an increasing desire for his kingdom and righteousness[153] (Matt 6:33) and a

---

150. Ruth, *Little Heaven Below*, 138–39.

151. Billman, *Supernatural Thread in Methodism*, 57–69.

152. Ruth, *Little Heaven Below*, 120.

153. Smith, *Desiring the Kingdom*, 133–51.

magnified expectancy of his supernatural work.[154] Moreover, Methodists will again come to expect and experience formation into growing sanctification and Christlikeness. The praxis of Constant Word and Sacrament will begin to impel Methodists to practice the other diverse means of grace as espoused by Wesley. As God changes minds and hearts, Methodists will desire to be more faithful in prayer, fasting, searching the Scriptures, Christian conferencing, etc. This includes gaining an increased desire to engage in various small groups for deeper Christian education (Sunday school, Bible studies, etc.) and for practical discipleship accountability (class meetings, covenant discipleship groups, etc.). It will initiate and enhance a cascade effect whereby each practiced means of grace will build on and feed off of one another. People will be challenged and driven, as Hamilton says, "to know, love, and serve God."[155] As a result, many Methodists will move toward a more radical Christian obedience.

Weems and Berlin assert that we become like what we worship and that divine fruit grows in the lives of people as the "overflow" of divine worship praxis.[156] This follows the precepts of Smith, who holds that it is through worship practices that God forms the desires of our hearts and develops in us a "Christian social imaginary" whereby we become in our living what we have come to desire in our being.[157]

Furthermore, as Billman evidences in *The Supernatural Thread*, many Methodists have already begun and will continue to increase in their desire for the fire of the Holy Spirit[158] and become more and more endowed with the full workings (gifts, fruits, etc.) of charismata.[159] The Sacrament has long been a "hot spot" among Methodists for charismatic encounters with the Holy Spirit,[160] including experiencing "the therapeutic effects of grace."[161]

---

154. Jennings, *Supernatural Occurrences of John Wesley*, 216; Ruth, *Little Heaven Below*, 161.

155. Hamilton, *Revival*, 87.

156. Weems and Berlin, *Overflow*, 10–13, 15–27.

157. Smith, *Desiring the Kingdom*, 18–19.

158. Billman, *Supernatural Thread in Methodism*, 103–14. Davies, *Spirit Baptism and Spiritual Gifts in Early Methodism*, 1–13.

159. Jennings, *Supernatural Occurrences of John Wesley*, 216–19; Nikodemos the Hagiorite, *Concerning Frequent Communion*, 104–5, 210–11. Davies, *Spirit Baptism and Spiritual Gifts in Early Methodism*, 1–13.

160. Billman, *Supernatural Thread in Methodism*, 61–62; Ruth, *Little Heaven Below*, 138–39.

161. Dayton, *Theological Roots of Pentecostalism*, 116–20.

Therapeutic grace is a very strong emphasis of Wesleyan practical divinity. In fact, following Dayton, Khoo says:

> The Wesleys utilised a therapeutic more than a legal framework to understand the divine-human interaction. Sin was seen as sickness, salvation as healing of this sickness, Christian formation as long-term spiritual therapy towards full healing and wholeness defined as 'Christian perfection.' To the Wesleys, Christian perfection is the goal of the Christian life. Referred to sometimes as 'entire sanctification,' 'scriptural holiness,' or 'perfect love,' Christian perfection simply means the state of living where there is 'holiness in heart and life,' where one loves God and one's neighbor with pure intention and where one becomes conformed to the image of Christ. It is with this understanding that the Wesleys saw the eucharist as a therapeutic Sacrament providing 'the medicine of immortality' for communicants as they seek to be healed of their present condition and become 'perfected in love.'[162]

Since Word and Sacrament is a direct encounter with the Triune God and the grand reception point for divine grace, it is also understood that one of the major effects of grace application is in divine healing.[163] Sin and resultant human fallenness manifests itself in all of the various ailments, degradations, and maladies of the current age. Yet, the increase of holiness stands in direct opposition to the symptomatic effects of fallenness. In the Wesleyan understanding, holiness and healing go hand-in-hand. Therefore, as Constant Word and Sacrament praxis is increased, the plain evidence of its efficacy through all sorts of divine healing—spiritual, physical, emotional, moral, ethical, relational, etc.—will no doubt also increase.

---

162. Khoo, *Wesleyan Eucharistic Spirituality*, 99. Khoo also refers to the Eucharist as "the healing Sacrament" and provides a fine short essay substantiating the Wesley's concurrence with that understanding (99–102). Also, note that Ignatius of Antioch (AD 30–107), an Ante-Nicene father (specifically an Apostolic Father, i.e., a student of one or more of the twelve apostles; in the case of Ignatius, he was a direct student of the apostle John) whose teachings were well known to Wesley, had previously described Holy Communion as "the medicine of immortality" in his Epistle to the Ephesians (c. AD 107). He also adds that it is "the antidote which prevents us from dying" and "a cleansing remedy driving away evil" (Ignatius, "Epistle of Ignatius," 1:57–58). The vast healing implications inherent to such images as "medicine," "antidote," and "remedy" are unmistakably straightforward. This message, securely rooted in the very early apostolic church, is that the sacramental therapy of Christ—grounded in the atonement of Christ—cures death and cleanses evil afflictions. The Wesleys and the early Methodists held strongly to this notion and dramatically experienced its visible reality. Why don't we?

163. Khoo, *Wesleyan Eucharistic Spirituality*, 55–107.

In light of such strong Christo-pneumatic interaction, the sacramental Table is the Pentecostal Table; it is a prime place where people can be especially receptive to any and all gifts of charismata; yet, as Khoo strongly asserts in true Wesleyan spirit: "The Sacrament is a place for healing."[164] This means it is the place for God to heal whatever needs to be healed, to give grace according to need, and to move people forward along the way of salvation towards an increasing Christlikeness. It also means that the more that Word and Sacrament is practiced in sustained fashion throughout our denomination, the more we will become availed of the work of God and the more that the Holy Spirit will strikingly touch hearts and lives and bring about widespread Pentecostal revival across the expanse of Methodism. The very kinds of things attested in Acts 2 and by the early Methodists—the miracles, signs, wonders, ecstatic gifts, mission impetus, and the greatly amplified salvation of souls—that is, this *work of God,* will come alive again in the ministries of contemporary United Methodism.[165] Divinely directed healing and missional power is readily available to our current sickly and diminished denomination. The key question is this: When will we again open ourselves to its mysterious and vigorous efficacy?

164. Khoo, *Wesleyan Eucharistic Spirituality,* 100; cf. Felton, *United Methodists and the Sacraments,* 56; and *This Holy Mystery,* 19–20.

165. Note that a prime biblical example of the Acts 2 church is the congregation at Corinth. In sequential concluding sections of his first letter to the Corinthians (ch. 16 is essentially a post-script), Paul connectively addresses first, the proper practice of Holy Communion (1 Cor 10–11), and then, immediately following, the proper practice of Holy Charismata (1 Cor 12–14); finally, he places it all in the context of the full and certain supernatural reality of the bodily resurrection of Christ (1 Cor 15). This topical sequencing is no mere coincidence. Just as the early Methodists rediscovered and experienced it again much later, the Corinthian Christians experienced the Sacrament of the Lord's Supper as a prime catalyst for the appearance and manifestation of the full range of charismatic gifts (via the Holy Spirit) for the missional purpose of "the common good" (1 Cor 12:7). Moreover, the empowering Source for this living *work of God* which occurred in and through the living church of God is none other than the living Host of the Table of God—the primordial Word and Sacrament himself—the risen Lord Jesus Christ. As they constantly encountered the risen Christ through Word and Sacrament, God made things happen. This is the actuality which enables Paul to conclude with these words: "But thanks be to God, who gives us the victory through our [risen] Lord Jesus Christ. Therefore, my beloved brethren, be steadfast, immovable, always abounding in the *work of the Lord,* knowing that in the Lord your labor is not in vain" (1 Cor 15:57–58). Like the Corinthians of the Acts 2 church and the early Methodists, this spiritual and missional potentiality is the same for us today. For we too are risen with Christ and are privy to the power of his resurrection (cf. 1 Pet 1; also, see Khoo, *Wesleyan Eucharistic Spirituality,* 62); and we Methodists have been brought into existence by God to be a complete restoration of the early apostolic (Pentecostal) church.

We are still yet alive. We have been bequeathed from Wesley with a divine methodology for the making of disciples. We have been powerfully endowed from God with an expectant faith and the optimism of grace. Thus, when the charismatic renewal occurs, the United Methodist Church will begin to experience healing and regain much of its missing power to go with its works of holiness.[166] This will also enhance the spiritual cascade effect. Following Wesley and Fletcher, Wood posits that true Methodism is a continued restoration of the apostolic and Pentecostal church.[167] There-fore, in the context of both White and Billman, as the renewed Pentecostal fire of the Spirit falls upon the people, especially through the medium of sacramental worship, all of God's gifts, fruits, and instituted practices will increasingly flourish and the salvific mission of United Methodism will dramatically come to life again and mightily expand.[168] Through having received a prophetic word of knowledge (1 Cor 12:8),[169] I am under deep conviction that God will cause these things to happen with our wholesale return to Constant Word and Sacrament praxis. Without question, Wilke speaks the prophetic truth:

> The United Methodist Church can burn again with the fires of Pentecost. The Holy Spirit can empower us to speak in all the languages of the world, can enable all women and men, old and young, of every race and nation to be inviting witnesses of peace, and can inflame the mission of Jesus Christ to save a lost and lonely world. We will [either] be consumed by fire or [be impassioned] by fire.[170]

166. Dayton, *Theological Roots of Pentecostalism*, 90–100.

167. Wood, *Meaning of Pentecost*, 56–58.

168. Weems and Berlin, *Overflow*, 10–13; Wood, *Meaning of Pentecost*, 151–58. Also, see Smith, *Evangelical, Sacramental & Pentecostal* (2017). Smith provides support for an integrated model of Christian emphasis: evangelical (focus on God's Word), sacramental (focus on God's Incarnation), and Pentecostal (focus on God's Spirit). He uses John 15:4 as the springboard of his understanding and avers that all three elements ("principles") are necessary. His overarching narrative, while commensurate with Wesleyan spirit, is slightly different in theory and practice. Whereas Smith advocates for three elements as foundational pillars, the Wesleyan model holds to the pillars of Word (evangelical emphasis) and Table (sacramental emphasis)—both held together as one entity—with the Pentecostal element not being an additional pillar, but rather a strong *spiritual result* of faithfully practicing Constant Word and Sacrament. The greatest ordinary medium of the Holy Spirit's activity is Word and Sacrament.

169. See 1 Corinthians 12:8–10. I have personally received multiple gifts of charis-mata from this particular inventory.

170. Wilke, *And are We Yet Alive?*, 124.

When will the renewal begin? That is the question that we as United Methodists have the opportunity to answer through our actions. As Wilke asserts above, we do have the capacity to set a new Pentecost into motion. It will not be through our own power, but through our acquiescence to the presence and power of God. The Spirit of God is even now ready to inaugurate the revival. In these last days, he is ready to pour himself out upon his people (Joel 2; Acts 2). God is waiting for the faithful and widespread return of Methodism to Constant Word and Sacrament worship.[171] When we do, the sleeping giant that is Methodism will become reawakened by the life-giving resurrection power of God and again spread gospel fire over the Earth.

Until then, however, we will continue to wither and die.

171. For a sense of the resurrection power of early Methodism as experienced through Word and Sacrament praxis, please note this entry by Charles Wesley in his *Journal* (Easter Sunday, April 14, 1745) as he makes reference to a service of worship: "Easter-day, April 14. With the word, the Spirit of Him that raised Jesus from the dead came mightily upon us. For more than half an hour He cried in our hearts. At the Sacrament, also, which the whole Society partook of, we all found, more or less, the power of His resurrection. So again at our love-feast, we rejoiced together, and felt that the Lord was risen indeed" (Wesley, *Journal of Charles Wesley*, 1:396). As Methodists, this reality is still available to us today and is, in fact, ours for the taking. The Wesleys recorded these events, not only for their own personal recollections, but so that their historic actualities would not be lost to future Methodist generations. It is at our peril that we continue to discard them.

4

The Practical Divinity in Action

> While God calls us, we must respond to that call. The decisions
> United Methodist clergy and laity must make in the period ahead
> will determine the future course, perhaps even the continued ex-
> istence, of United Methodism. We are convinced that God is still
> calling The United Methodist Church to witness and to serve, to
> "spread scriptural holiness throughout the land." The response is
> up to us.[1]

In the renowned movie, *Wesley: A Heart Transformed Can Change the World* (2009), there is an early scene where John and Charles Wesley are making one of their regular visits to Bocardo Prison and providing bread to the indigent captives. As they are offering bread to the hungry people, one particular prisoner, somewhat belligerently, gets in John's face and tells him that what he is doing is making no real difference at all. As they are leaving, Charles remarks to John, "He's right, you know. We could build charity schools, almshouses for the poor, and give our time and money to others, but in the end, it really doesn't change very much." And John responds, "Yes, but we must try, Charles. We must ensure our own salvation, if nothing else." To that, Charles, with weak resignation, says, "Yes—we must try."[2]

---

1. Willimon and Wilson, *Rekindling the Flame*, 127.
2. Jackman, *Wesley*.

Thankfully, that was not the end of the Wesleyan story. Following Aldersgate in May 1738, long after the charitable, yet somewhat futile faith strivings of the Wesleys (as portrayed in the above movie scene) finally became intermixed with the transformative grace and Pentecostal power of God, an aging and reflective John—looking back upon the mighty work of God in the past decades of the Revival—could astoundingly proclaim in April 1777, "What hath God wrought!"[3] In Wesley's understanding, the Methodist reclamation of the divinely ordained practices of the Acts 2 church had unleashed the work of God and dramatically impacted the world parish for the cause of Christ.[4]

In the years since the Wesleys, a dire ecclesial irony has developed. The Methodist Revival has become itself in great need of a Methodist Revival. This is especially tragic because we United Methodists are hungering in the midst of plenty.[5] It is by our own choice that we do not regularly eat the sumptuous divine feast of grace that the Lord has put before us.[6]

It is our contention that the congregations of United Methodism are spiritually subsisting on a diet of regular servings of Word, but with very meager helpings of Sacrament. Thus, we are no longer experiencing "the full, rich and joyous eucharistic [Word *and* Sacrament] life of early Methodists."[7]

---

3. Wesley, "On Laying the Foundation," 3:579–92.

4. Wesley, "Journal" (October 28, 1762), 21:392.

5. It is interesting to note that my own conference, the North Carolina Annual Conference, is often considered to be one of the healthiest of the UMC conferences in America. However, that notwithstanding, while we are not yet experiencing the extreme symptoms of other annual conferences, we too are languidly suffering the subtle effects of spiritual malnourishment. For instance, during the period from 2012 to 2015, the NCC showed total losses in both membership (231,269 to 228,611 = -2,658) and in worship attendance (79,743 to 74,450 = -5,293) (Statistical data retrieved from http://journal.nccumc.org/). In recent years, this has been the trend of the NCC: slow but steady erosion in total membership coupled with a slightly more visible drop in worship participation. Sadly, this reveals an especially un-Wesleyan current reality, for these numbers also show that only about 1/3 of the total membership regularly attend services of worship. At best, we are barely treading water; at worst, we are slowly sinking. The obvious question is, then, what about those many other conferences who are *less healthy* than the NCC? In all honesty, this really means that, as a whole, the UMC in America is and has long been spiritually sick unto death with some annual conferences merely dying slower than other annual conferences.

6. See à Kempis, *Imitation of Christ*, 309–10.

7. Chilcote, *Recapturing the Wesleys' Vision*, 84.

Allow me to use an analogy. It would be an unfortunate thing to walk hungry into a posh steak house expecting to get a large ribeye, an all-you-can-eat salad bar, and a large baked potato with all the trimmings, only to receive a tiny meat morsel, a small cup of salad, and a dinner roll. The food might be good, but one will surely walk away unsatisfied. Now, imagine having a similar experience with every meal—week after week after week. Sadly, that is exactly how it is as to the ongoing spiritual well-being of many Methodists. On most Sundays of the year, the sermon may provide some nourishment to the soul, but without also the Sacrament, that soul remains woefully underfed. The degree of spiritual atrophy magnifies with each passing week. Both the individual congregant and the collective congregation suffer persisting loss with little reprieve from starvation. Over time, the atrophy becomes chronic—and routine—and perhaps for a long while, even unrecognized. Initially, there is the loss of divine expectancy; then a loss of committed discipleship. Some people may fall away from the faith entirely. The mission of the church degrades. An inward focus ensues and a desperate survival mode kicks in. Pastors, truly called of God, become discouraged—some even to the point of no return who finally just throw in their holy cloth once and for all. Likewise, some of the local churches may give up the fight and close their doors; yet, many more just continue to exist, going through the ritualistic motions, hopelessly hanging on for dear life. Does any of this sound familiar?[8]

Today, many congregations practice the Sacrament in only monthly increments and on certain other special days. Still other local churches only celebrate quarterly or even less. In terms of Wesleyan standards, such a level of consumption is not the nutritionally balanced spiritual diet recommended for Methodists in the fulfillment of Wesleyan discipleship development.[9] As such, we find ourselves nibbling only on the crumbs that fall from the Master's table instead of feasting on "the fullness of immortal bread"[10] that Jesus says is abundantly available in him (John 6:35–36, 49–51; 1 Cor

8. Alas! There are some pastors and congregations who may claim to be doing well without the administration of Constant Communion. So, they ask, why bother tinkering with something that is not broken? Because it *is* broken. The presence of any *doing well* simply means that God is still operating *in spite* of us. To those folks, please know this: the spiritual malnourishment still exists; yet, just imagine what God would then do if both of his Tables of grace were in service, at least, every Sunday. The work of God would magnify exponentially.

9. Chilcote, *Recapturing the Wesleys' Vision*, 80–81.

10. Maddox, "Hymns," 39:54:3–4.

10:16–17). Moreover, we consequentially find ourselves not profusely making disciples of Jesus Christ for the transformation of the world. Why do The People Called Methodists not constantly avail themselves of the fullness of God's free grace, especially when, as Wesley said, "the benefits of doing it are so great?"[11] That is a question for the ages.

We must remember that while monthly Communion is better than quarterly Communion, even monthly service is only about 25 percent of Wesley's minimum prescription.[12] Note that Wesley himself took the Sacrament at least once a week for most of his life and an average of four to five times a week during the years of the Methodist-Evangelical Revival.[13] As we are his spiritual progeny, Wesley's practice is quite instructive for us. We must never forget Wesley's teaching that "All who desire to increase in the grace of God are to wait for it in partaking of the Lord's Supper."[14] Nor should we dismiss the admonition of Senn: "We cannot ignore the fact that the specific and concrete way in which we experience the real presence of Christ is in Holy Communion."[15]

The good news, we believe, is that a simple correction is all that it would take to recover the authentic Wesleyan way and begin restoring Methodism to the passionate worshipping and vibrant missional community we were created to be. However, the reality, we fear, is that the simple correction will not be so easily made. Some pastors will inevitably resist. Many congregations will do the same. But, oh, what God can bring about yet again with a faithful return to Constant Word and Sacrament praxis!

11. Wesley, "Duty of Constant Communion," 3:429.

12. As another illustration, we are talking about the church equivalent of a V-8 engine running on the power and effectiveness of (usually) only two to four, or occasionally five, of its eight cylinders. If the engine runs at all, it is dramatically weakened. In many of our local churches, the "Word pistons" are busy working away while the "Sacrament pistons" remain largely idle. Yet, unlike with a motor vehicle, it is an easy fix. We do not have to completely rebuild the engine; we can just decide to start using the inactive pistons again. In effect, this is precisely what the Wesleys did in their day to first inaugurate renewal, and then to keep growing and maintaining the Methodist-Evangelical Revival. We can do the very same today.

13. Felton, *This Holy Mystery*, 11; cf. Chilcote, *Recapturing the Wesleys' Vision*, 84. Here Chilcote specifically asserts that Wesley took Communion "on an average of once every four days throughout his lifetime."

14. Wesley, "Means of Grace," 1:389.

15. Senn, *Stewardship of the Mysteries*, 30.

The Need for Courageous Pastoral Leadership

A recent study (2015) of the pastors-in-charge in one annual conference[16] revealed an interesting paradox. According to the data, over two-thirds of the pastors surveyed (in fact, nearly seven out of ten) indicated a very high sacramental understanding of Holy Communion.[17] Specifically, this understanding included the notions that the Sacrament serves as a fountain of spiritual nourishment and growing sanctification, a point of spiritual unity with God and one another, and as a special catalyst for receiving new spiritual gifts, blessings, and even divine healing according to need. These pastors also highly indicated that they believed the Sacrament should be practiced as often as possible because of the life-changing and transformative benefits which God gives through it. However, here is the paradox. Less than one in ten of those very same pastors celebrate Holy Communion weekly in their local churches.[18] This begs the obvious question: Why is there such a great discrepancy between the high sacramental understanding of Holy Communion efficacy purportedly held by so many Methodist pastors and the admitted lack of sacramental administration frequency practiced by the same pastors? Among those who claim to be a part of the Wesleyan tradition, this practical reality is indeed a bit bizarre and troublesome. In fact, Wesley himself also commented on the strangeness of such a rampant sacramental neglect within the church:

> It is no wonder that men who have no fear of God should never think of doing this. But it is strange that it should be neglected by any that do fear God, and desire to save their souls. And yet nothing is more common.[19]

In effect, Wesley likened this neglect of Constant Holy Communion praxis to being a non-Christian *inaction* that is sadly quite common among professing Christians and local churches. He also emphatically added: "We must neglect no occasion which the good providence of God affords us for

16. For anyone who may be interested, the detailed results of this study can be found in my doctoral dissertation, *Necessity of Constant Word and Sacrament,* 131–58. It is available from the Theological Research Exchange Network (www.tren.com). While this survey data is specific to the North Carolina Annual Conference, we believe that it is also a microcosm of empirical evidence pointing to a greater denomination-wide endemic of sacramental neglect.

17. Stallings, *Necessity of Constant Word and Sacrament,* 134.

18. Stallings, *Necessity of Constant Word and Sacrament,* 156–57.

19. Wesley, "Duty of Constant Communion," 3:428.

this purpose. This is the true rule—so often are we to receive as God gives us opportunity."[20]

In making such a strong assertion, Wesley, in effect, is making sacramental accessibility into a pastoral matter. First, it is pastoral because it has prominent soteriological linkage. It is the "grand channel" of grace of which God uses to sanctify people and move them further along the *Ordo salutis*, i.e., the way of salvation. Second, it is also pastoral because it serves as a grand statement of faith renewal each time people submit themselves to God at the altar. It is both faith building and faith sustaining. Oden bluntly avers: "Where the Eucharistic meal is not celebrated, the laity are not being nurtured as the body of Christ."[21] This succinctly places sacramental administration within the realm of the most significant pastoral care; and all pastors should have the highest of concern for the uttermost salvation, transformation, and faith development of their congregants.

Of course, this pastoral element puts the impetus and responsibility firmly in the hands of those of us who are the pastors of the local churches. We should take the reins of leadership (which we all willfully accepted upon our taking of holy orders) and be faithful to this true rule. For it is the pastors who provide the people with the opportunity to receive the Sacrament and its benefits. Unless we offer it constantly, our people cannot receive it constantly. Woe be unto us when we, as the under-shepherds of Christ, fail our sheep in this regard. Thus, there is a need for a pragmatic Word-Sacrament re-balancing in our services of worship in order for people to achieve continued positive and maturing growth in Christ. Just as we, as pastors, will be held accountable for the content of our didactic ministry (Jas 3:1),[22] so will we also be held accountable for the stewardship of our sacramental ministry (1 Cor 4:1–4).[23] In every way, we have been made special stewards of God's grace for a salvific purpose.

We will now share two practical principles of sacramental stewardship. First, there is the *Just Do it* Principle. And, second, there is the *Just Teach it* Principle.

---

20. Wesley, "Duty of Constant Communion," 3:429.

21. Oden, *Classic Christianity*, 718.

22. Willimon and Wilson, *Rekindling the Flame*, 80–87.

23. Senn, *Stewardship of the Mysteries*, 2–3.

The *Just Do it* Principle

There remains a good foundation for the potential recovery of Constant Word and Sacrament praxis in our churches. After all, as long as God is still God, as long as the Holy Scriptures remain unchanged by God, and as long as Methodism continues to be endowed with the sacramental teachings of the Wesleys, then the call from God to utilize Constant Word and Sacrament in our local Methodist churches does not and will not change. We affirm that all of the above are still in full force and effect.

Therefore, with God's command to commune still proclaimed, and with God's presence and God's power still available, it is quite unnecessary that many of our local United Methodist congregations—the progeny of the sacramental Wesleys—are not experiencing the fullness of God's grace, especially through, of all things, a general neglect of the Sacrament of Holy Communion. In conversations with pastors and other church leaders over the years, perhaps the most frequent reason mentioned for its flagging implementation is that their congregations are just "not ready" for Constant Communion.[24] After a quarter century in the pastoral ministry, we must confess to having grown wary of the phrase "not ready." It is not a valid response. It is merely an excuse used to avoid taking a necessary kingdom action. Interestingly, this is the same phrase that has been used so many times from various local churches as an excuse to avoid potentially receiving a female or other minority pastor. With deeply entrenched cultural mores, including sometimes overt sexism and racism, in place—although such prejudices are still grievously wrong—one can more easily understand the sinful "not ready" congregational response to certain pastoral appointments. But why to Communion? What sort of *prejudice* can there be toward the practice of Constant Holy Communion? Is there really a congregation out there that actually has a problem with continuously communing with Christ, who is our Savior? Let's be real. What is it about Constant Holy Communion that causes someone to say they are "not ready" for it? If it is okay to serve Holy Communion at all, whether occasionally, quarterly, or even monthly, then what is the great barrier to offering it every Sunday? There is certainly no black magic attached to the notion; and it is highly doubtful that, with Constant Communion, some popish boogeyman is going to jump out of the cup, or that the bread is going to suddenly turn into

---

24. See Wesley, "Duty of Constant Communion," 3:428–39, for his responses to the most common excuses.

the Blob and consume everyone. Think about it. The sheer ludicrousness of these images parallels the sheer ludicrousness of the "not ready" excuse.

There is nothing whatsoever about Constant Communion of which to be fearful, or to have any sort of dark suspicion. Holy Communion is a Sacrament of grace instituted of God. As such, Wesley called it both "the blessed Sacrament"[25] and "the grand channel whereby the grace of his Spirit was conveyed to the souls of all the children of God."[26] Do we not want or need to receive as much divine blessing and grace as possible? An answer in the negative is absurd. So, what's *really* the problem here?

Furthermore, as Wesley reminded people in his sermon, "The Duty of Constant Communion," the Lord commanded the church to "do this" (Luke 22:19), so why should not Christians seek to obey his commandments as often as possible?[27] Wesley was right on the mark, for as the apostle John asserted, keeping the Lord's commandments is a demonstration of our love for him and even of our love for his church (1 John 5:1–5).[28] The logic of merely an occasional obedience is also absurd. For instance, would we apply the same reasoning to the Ten Commandments; that is, to only see fit to obey them quarterly or perhaps just once a month? If not, why are we so remiss about our constant obedience to the Communion Commandment?

Another thought: What about preaching? How would a local congregation respond to a pastor who desires to administer Communion every Sunday, but only to preach a sermon quarterly or once a month?[29] In the Wesleyan tradition, either such omission is tantamount to being the

---

25. Wesley, "Duty of Constant Communion," 3:430.

26. Wesley, "Upon Our Lord's Sermon on the Mount," 1:585.

27. Wesley, "Duty of Constant Communion," 3:431. Here he says, "Are we not to obey every command of God as often as we can?"

28. In his sermon, "Witness of the Spirit I" (1746), Wesley spoke of the connection between our love of God and our obedience to God: "Once more, the Scriptures teach, 'This is the love of God (the sure mark thereof) that we keep his commandments.' And our Lord himself saith, 'He that keepeth my commandments, he it is that loveth me.' Love rejoices to obey, to do in every point whatever is acceptable to the Beloved. A true lover of God hastens to do his will on earth as it is done in heaven" (Wesley, "Witness of the Spirit I," 1:280). This is a constantly recurring theme throughout Wesley's writings and thus throughout his practical divinity. It is a premise that he applies specifically to the ongoing practice of Constant Holy Communion (Wesley, "Duty of Constant Communion," 3:428–29, 431–32).

29. I cannot help but laugh at the thought of a pastor announcing that next Sunday is "Sermon Sunday"!

same thing.[30] So, again, why do we typically place one admonition of God ("preach the word") higher than the other admonition ("do this")? Both are the Wesleyan *True Rule*.

Our response to "not ready" churches is to just get ready by making it happen now. In fact, from personal pastoral experience, we have found that the best way to get ready is to just start doing it. The work of God will then be unleashed in new and powerful ways, including in the transformation (sometimes dramatic!) of individual people and entire local congregations. A resistance to Constant Communion is itself the evidence of a need for further discipleship development. In this regard, Willimon presents a sure irony when he avers that "sacramental rigors . . . became life-long, distinctive characteristics of Wesley's approach to Christian formation."[31] This implies that resistance to these "sacramental rigors" is actually a barrier to making disciples (a task which, be reminded, is *the* mission of The United Methodist Church.)

Such resistance will not simply go away on its own. It requires a proactive pastoral response. Thus, for Christian formation to again become prolific, the cycle of resistance to those Wesleyan things that lead to Christian formation must be broken. Therefore, as pastors, it is imperative that we just do it.[32] Constant Communion is, after all, not merely a human act, but a supernatural God event in which humans co-participate. In the midst of our just doing it, we can be sure that God will do his work through it[33]—including even the softening of the hearts of those who, for whatever reason, may oppose.

---

30. Wesley, "Farther Appeal to Men," 8:62. He affirms: "There is no manner of need to set the one in opposition to the other; seeing we continually exhort all who attend on our preaching to attend the offices of the Church." He is stressing the need for Word *and* Sacrament; there is no conflict between the two, but rather the necessity for *both*. Attendance to the Methodist preaching, whether in the field, the chapel, or elsewhere, is not in itself enough. One should also attend the Sacrament as well, which typically means Lord's Day worship in the local parish sanctuary.

31. Willimon and Wilson, *Rekindling the Flame*, 38.

32. And, yes, this does mean with the same courage and staunch resolution as displayed by Admiral David Farragut with his reported, "Damn the torpedoes! Full speed ahead!" This is truly a sacred hill worthy of dying on.

33. White, *Sacraments as God's Self Giving*, 59–61. He proclaims: "The Church is where the Spirit acts, and the eucharist is the center of the Church's life together" (60). This is precisely what we are largely missing.

The *Just Teach it* Principle

After (or even simultaneously with) the immediate implementation of the *Just Do it* Principle, we recommend the quick implementation of the *Just Teach it* Principle, as well. We have found that teaching the Wesleyan theological foundations of Constant Communion are best achieved along with the implementation of the practice of Constant Communion itself. Likewise, the implementation of the practice is best accompanied by the thorough teaching of its theological underpinnings. This bit of pragmatics, by the way, is simply an example of Word and Sacrament in cooperative action. It is itself Wesleyan practical divinity.

It is also quite notable that the visible impact of sacramental efficacy in individuals and in congregations is usually more overt when praxis and teaching are continuously commensurate with one another. Merely teaching about the merits of Constant Communion will not alone produce any merits from Communion; the Sacrament itself must also be practiced. It is quite logical that the more it is used, the more impact it will have, and that the less it is used, the less impact it will have. Furthermore, teaching about those merits and their inherent impacts while also practicing Constant Communion will deepen our awareness of God's action and often cause even the subtle aspects of the work of God to come more into plain view. The sustained usage of the Sacrament along with its continual teaching provides for mutual reinforcement and complimentary support.

Note further that we do not teach the foundations of Constant Communion merely to convince people of its rote validity and thus to lessen any opposition to it among the people of the congregation; most importantly, we teach it to spiritually edify and nurture the people of the congregation. Any necessary lessening of opposition comes with the deepening of sanctification. Sanctification occurs both in the growing of our essential understanding and in the changing of our essential being. The Holy Spirit is at work in us holistically throughout the process. In all Wesleyan teaching and practices, the goal is *always* for the progression of Christian sanctification and ultimately for the attainment of perfect Christlikeness (John 17:17–19; cf. 2 Pet 3:18).[34]

---

34. Willimon and Wilson, *Rekindling the Flame*, 40–41. Here they state: "In stressing sanctification—Christian formation—Wesley wedded the Protestant stress on justification with the Roman Catholic stress on holy living. Instantaneous new birth is followed by a lifelong process of sanctification. John Wesley asserted the value of regular participation in the corporate worship of the church through prayer, Bible reading, fasting,

The Final Exhortation

We believe that the most important application is the facilitation of the proper re-balancing of Word and Sacrament in the worship life and spirituality of United Methodist congregations. Many empirical indicators strongly confirm this need. Yet, the need for re-balancing is far more than a reformation of worship methodology; it is also the recovery of a proven system of Christian discipleship development. While acceptable Christian worship is certainly for the glory of God, it is also for the benefit of the people of God in our growth in sanctification toward perfection and ultimate Christlikeness. As Smith has said, "worship is the center of gravity of the task of discipleship."[35] In Wesleyan practical divinity, the event of divine Word and Sacrament worship is understood to be the grandest of all spiritual disciplines because it is the greatest transformative encounter of all with God-in-Christ.[36] It is the sustained encounter dynamic of divine worship that is the key element in its transformative efficacy. In other words, the more we engage in the sacramental presence of God, the more we are sacramentally changed by God by being in his presence. Through his sacramental presence, God effects his beneficial self-giving.[37] As God gives himself to us, we become more transformed into his likeness and become more like the people he wants us to be.

The Christians of the early apostolic church both understood this efficacious process and practiced it through Constant Word and Sacrament worship. This is seen in the foundational Scripture texts used for this study (Acts 2:42–43, 46–47; 1 Tim 4:14–16; 1 Cor 10:16–17, 11:23–26). Likewise,

---

Christian conference, and the Lord's Supper. This is in contrast to some Protestants of his day (and our own), because these 'ordinary means of grace,' as Wesley called the Sacraments and the church, strengthen and perfect us. . . . Confident that they had experienced a reality greater than that of the world, these Methodists sought to embody and to inculcate the Spirit of Christ, to make people who, in their daily living, resembled Christ."

35. Smith, *Desiring the Kingdom*, 213.

36. Cherry, *Worship Architect*, 16–17; cf. 25–28; Schmemann, *For the Life*, 26–28; Khoo, *Wesleyan Eucharistic Spirituality*, 180–82.

37. White, *Sacraments as God's Self Giving*, 61. He states: "Christ, as the underlying Sacrament on which all Sacraments are based, gives himself to us most directly to us in this [the Lord's Supper] Sacrament. We remember his sacrifice and all his other works on our behalf until the end of time, express our thanksgiving, are united to one another, and experience the Holy Spirit as he makes Christ's presence known to us. If it all seems very complicated, it is also beautifully simple, perceptible to the least sophisticated. Here Christ gives himself anew to us just as he once did for all in the Incarnation."

Wesley, in and through the Methodist-Evangelical Revival, instigated a renewal of the Acts 2 church discipleship processes through his use of the same Word and Sacrament practices.[38] This is clearly heard in his sermons and other writings, but even more powerfully, it is clearly demonstrated by his actions.

In this same spirit, Borgen is immediately instructive. He stresses that "a recovery of Wesley's basic emphases is urgently needed."[39] We have become a hotbed of loose-cannon theology and loose-cannon practices. Our longtime departure from the methodical system of Wesleyanism has led to a demise of discipleship in the United Methodist Church.[40] We are not notably fulfilling our mission and are in grave need of again recovering the same Acts 2 apostolic power and disciple-making capacity that once made Methodism a salvific machine.[41] We believe that this will come only through a general return to the sustained Word and Sacrament practices of Wesleyan spirituality.[42]

There seems to be several current realities among Methodist pastors and churches. While the usage of the Word seems to be good, there are some major issues with the usage of the Sacrament. A high number of pastors seem to adhere to a strong sacramental *means of grace* understanding of Holy Communion. Moreover, a correlative number of them also believe that the administration of Holy Communion, when used, currently produces a positive impact in their local churches. Yet, the actual practice of Holy Communion in the local parishes seems to be very minimal.

In summation, according to both Wesleyan teaching and the notions of many Methodist pastors, there is great power and benefit inherent to Word and Sacrament praxis. Yet, Word is practiced constantly in the local

38. Chilcote, *Recapturing the Wesleys' Vision*, 80; cf. Rattenbury, *Wesley's Legacy to the World*, 173–95.

39. Borgen, *John Wesley on the Sacraments*, 281.

40. See Willimon and Wilson, *Rekindling the Flame*, 41. They state: "Wesley knew enough about human nature and the nature of the gospel to know that no individual alone can sustain this hope, can embody the Christian life-style. Therefore, he created structures of corporate life [the Methodist Society system], which enabled the Methodists to produce the sort of disciples they believed the gospel deserved. In salvation, God takes the initiative in reaching out to us in Jesus Christ. But we must respond through a concrete, communal embodiment of our response to God's initiative."

41. Payne, *American Methodism*, 17; cf. Wilke, *And are We Yet Alive?*, 79: "If our church is to be reborn, it must experience once again the life of the early church."

42. See the chart at the end of this chapter: "A Wesleyan-Methodist Model for Making Disciples in the Local Church."

parishes, but not Sacrament. In our estimation, there appears to be a predominant understanding present that is commensurate with rote (cognitive) Wesleyan theology, but contradictory in its actual implementation. A great disconnect exists. Since Wesleyan theology must always be translated into praxis in order to be authentic, then the fullness of Wesley's practical divinity is not widespread in our churches. For the sake of our Christian mission to make disciples of Jesus Christ for the transformation of the world, this requires swift correction.

We have suggested three simple steps for our single-focus United Methodist revitalization. They will be mentioned briefly here as part of a concluding review.

Step One: We should retrain our sacramental understanding. Beginning with our pastors and then moving outward to the general body of laity, a strong sacramental understanding of existence should be taught and thoroughly inculcated. The Scriptures, as well as our Wesleyan-Methodist tradition, are staunchly sacramental in their theological foundations. Over time, we have lost much of that understanding. Due to long-term denominational amnesia spawned by such things as the impact of American frontier evangelicalism (with its de-emphasis on the necessity of Holy Communion), by Enlightenment and naturalistic philosophical incursions (with their de-emphasis on the activity of the supernatural), and by the subsumed influences of many transfers into Methodism from non-sacramental traditions (bringing with them an inherent unawareness of the deep and active relationship between Word-Sacrament and the supernatural), our theology and our practices have gradually become exceedingly diluted by other streams of influence. Unwittingly, we as a denomination have functionally given up much of our divine sacramental weight and have become much more Pelagian than Wesleyan-Arminian.[43] (Even our preaching is often reflective of this; many sermons today are much more human-centered and irresolute than Wesley's God-driven "Thus saith the Lord.") In general, through its long and widespread absence, we have lost a great sense of our

---

43. See Felton, *This Holy Mystery*, 7. She states: "According to the results of a survey conducted by the General Board of Discipleship prior to the 2000 General Conference, there is a strong sense of the importance of Holy Communion in the life of individual Christians and of the church. Unfortunately, there is at least an equally strong sense of absence of any meaningful understanding of Eucharistic theology and practice. United Methodists recognize that grace and spiritual power are available to them in the Sacrament, but too often they do not feel enabled to receive these gifts and apply them in their lives." And, sadly, all these years later, this sacramental inaccessibility—whether instigated by indifference or resistance—is *still* the case in many of our congregations.

divine sacramentality. In so doing, we have actually eased into a latent form of Gnosticism and have suffered a grave disconnect in our mission and ministry from the power and authority of the bodily Risen Christ of the Scriptures (cf. Matt 28:16–20; Acts 1–2), who has chosen primarily to work his wonders through certain *physical* signs.[44]

There are many of us, including pastors, who—though we may give some form of cognitive assent—do not seem to fully grasp at the deepest possible (heart) magnitude the veracity and critical necessity of Wesleyan Word and Sacrament theology. In fact, concerning the clergy, there are many of us who have simply been insufficiently exposed to such a Wesleyan teaching, and others of us who have not yet reached the point of total heart conviction concerning its veracity. This, of course, includes our historic teaching about the interactive, dynamic, and unitive relationship that exists between the proclamation of the Word (inclusive of the public readings of Scripture, as well as its fervent preaching and teaching) and the administration of the Sacrament, whereby the maximal opportunity for congregants to receive God's grace is provided. Without it, we have aligned ourselves to a significant degree with an anti-supernatural faith. As Borgen observes, "later [contemporary] Methodism has paid dearly for tearing apart what God has united."[45] This trend needs to be reversed. Our sacramental view

44. After discussing the inferences of the Pauline image of the church being called the *body* of Christ (55–56), Rattenbury then asks a penetrating question which confronts head-on the subtle and stealthy Gnosticism of non-sacramental Christianity: "Is it not possible that He [Jesus], really present in our midst, can use material things like bread and wine as He used his material body to fulfill His mission? His body was the instrument of His spirit. Is it not true that the bread and the wine are abiding instruments of His spirit for the feeding of the souls of men?" (Rattenbury, *Thoughts on Holy Communion*, 56). In our disregard of constant sacramental praxis, we are indeed gnostically disregarding, as Rattenbury implies, the "abiding [material] instruments of His [Christ's] spirit." Such disregard is neither Wesleyan nor biblical; Wesley's revulsion, for instance, for quietism was essentially a revulsion for functional Gnosticism, particularly the Docetic variation. Practical sacramentalism, grounded in the incarnation and resurrection of Christ, refutes *all* forms of Gnosticism. In fact, both the incarnation and resurrection of Christ, in the most basal way, are about spirituality as manifested through physicality. Sacramentalism is a simple extension of that same *work of God*. Wesley and his early progeny knew this well and utilized it to the salvific maximum.

45. Borgen, *John Wesley on the Sacraments*, 282. His whole statement is as follows: "Wesley refused extremes, but always maintained what was essential. He had one goal: to spread scriptural holiness over the world, by *all means*. There is, therefore, no need to set, for instance, the Word and preaching in opposition to the Sacraments. Wesley demanded both. The distinction between 'evangelicalism' and 'sacramentalism' must never be applied to Wesley. For him these two aspects were one, and later Methodism has paid dearly

must be deepened and heightened and vociferously demonstrated. Every primary worship service should be built upon the premise that the proclamation of the Word (Word-in-text: Holy Scripture) will always culminate in the administration of the Sacrament (Word-at-table: Holy Communion). Such is historic Wesleyan-Methodist worship that represents "the whole liturgy" concept[46] rather than a partial and lesser liturgy. Senn reminds us of what this means:

> Regular participation in the liturgy of the Word anchors one in the faith of Christ by rehearsing the story of our salvation in a systematic way through the observances of the church-year calendar and the structure of the lectionary. In the liturgy of the eucharistic meal (or Holy Communion, or the Lord's Supper) the faithful receive Christ himself, his body and blood in the form of bread and wine to connect us with Christ himself, forgive our sins, nourish us in his new life, and give us a foretaste of the feast to come.[47]

Anything less than the whole liturgy unfortunately smacks of an anthropocentric bent which is indicative of nondependence upon Christocentric sacramental grace.[48]

The bottom line is that we have experienced a tragic failure to utilize proven and potent "two-edged" Wesleyan pragmatics.[49] There is an urgent and pressing need for clergy to be much more intentionally exposed to the richness of Wesleyan sacramentalism, both theologically and pragmatically. This exposure should begin at the very earliest point of our seminary ministerial preparation. We suggest that it should then continue throughout our career through uniform and regular in-service teaching at the district level.[50] Just as it was with the Wesleys and the early Methodists,

---

for tearing apart what God has united."

46. Chan, *Liturgical Theology*, 66.

47. Senn, *Stewardship of the Mysteries*, 30–31.

48. Knight, *Presence of God*, 167–69.

49. Chilcote, *Recapturing the Wesleys' Vision*, 80–85.

50. See Felton, *This Holy Mystery*, 7. She adds this: "Many laypeople complain of sloppy practice, questionable theology, and lack of teaching and guidance. Both clergy and laity recognize the crucial need for better education of pastors in sacramental theology and practice. The concern for improved education is coupled with a call for accountability. Bishops, district superintendents, and other annual conference and general church authorities are urged to prepare their pastors better and to hold them accountable for their sacramental theology, practice, and teaching. Many of the people surveyed are plainly resentful of the lack of leadership they believe they are receiving in these areas.

our supermajority thinking (leading to our supermajority practicing) must again become intensely sacramental.

Step Two: We should implement a Wesleyan-biblical delivery system. Some form of the classic Word and Table liturgy should be utilized in all of our local churches because it sets forth in our worship a biblical conversational pattern of divine self-giving and human response.[51]

Just as a firsthand example, in the order of worship at my current local church (Lucama United Methodist Church in Lucama, North Carolina), we have converted to the following fourfold variation: [1] Our Gathering to God's Call; [2] Our Encounter with God's Word and Sacrament; [3] Our Response to God's Word and Sacrament; and [4] Our Sending Forth as God's People. We use this ordering of "Word and Table" because it emphasizes not only the divine self-giving and human response, but also stresses much more strongly the essential unity and inseparability of Word and Sacrament. There are, however, a number of effectual "Word and Table" four-step formats that can be used.

To be truly Wesleyan in our method, the proclamation of the Scriptures (Word-in-text) and the administration of Holy Communion (Word-at-table) should be practiced every Sunday in the primary service of worship. This will provide for a continuous maximal encounter of the people with Christ, who is the eternal Living Word (John 1:1–17 = *logos*), which will in turn provide for the maximal transfer of his transforming grace to the people (v. 16: "And from his fullness we have all received grace upon grace"; cf. 2 Cor 3:18[52]). Since historic Methodism is strongly focused upon the ongoing increase of sanctification via the means of sacramental grace, the recovery and use of this delivery system is imperative.[53]

Step Three: We should unleash the work of God. Wesleyan sacramental worship is not merely the practice of a certain system of stagnant rites. It is a living worship that connects people in a responsive relational encounter with the living God.[54] As we come to understand that we indeed live in a

---

These results are troubling and must provoke the church to reexamination and recommitment." And, sadly, all these years later, this lack of sacramental leadership commitment is also *still* the case in many of our congregations.

51. Cherry, *Worship Architect*, 8–9, 15.

52. 2 Cor 3:18—"And we all, with unveiled face, beholding the glory of the Lord, are being changed into his likeness from one degree of glory to another; for this comes from the Lord who is the Spirit."

53. Job, *Three Simple Rules*, 53–54; cf. Schillebeeckx, *Christ the Sacrament*, 182.

54. Cherry, *Worship Architect*, 8–9. Here she states: "God's saving acts were acts of

sacramental universe in which God ordinarily chooses to work supernaturally through the natural things that he has made, including through such mundane things as a sacred book, the bread and the wine, the people who make up the church, etc.,[55] the more that we will be open and unresistant to, and expectant of, the full power and benefit of our encounters with him. God wants us to fulfill our mission of making disciples (Matt 28:18–20)[56] and he wants us to fully utilize his capacity to do so through us[57] (cf. Acts 1:1–8, 2:1–4, 42–47). The work of God was mightily unleashed in the Acts 2 church and once again in the Methodist-Evangelical Revival. It can also happen today in an even greater demonstration of divine glory and power as we expectantly and optimistically *wait upon God* by devoting ourselves "to the apostles' teaching and fellowship, to the breaking of bread and the prayers" (Acts 2:42). It is through such means that God can and will make all things new.[58]

We are certain that there is already a foundation in place for the practice of Constant Communion to eventually become just as widespread as is Constant Word. Yet, it needs significant deepening and expansion, for our current praxis of Holy Communion is still far from Wesleyan standards. What we need is for those of us who are pastors to cast away any and

self-revelation. . . . Notice, however, that God's action invites a response. . . . 'Worship is the response we make to the gifts of God.' . . . The reciprocity inherent in a true worship experience is a beautiful thing in which to participate; it is a living, vital conversation, not a religious program. . . . True worship is the experience of encountering God."

55. Chauvet, *Sacraments*, 153. He describes this supernatural, extraordinary, divine grace given to us through the natural ordinary (a book, bread and drink) as the "paradox of the most divine given within the most human."

56. Payne, *American Methodism*, ix.

57. Felton, *This Holy Mystery*, 11; also, in *United Methodists and the Sacraments*, she provides this reminder of the sacramental-evangelistic-missional connection: "Holy Communion prepares us for and propels us into mission. The grace that we have received is to be used in work in the world toward conditions of justice and peace. We are charged to continue Christ's work of redeeming the world" (56). Further, we best not forget the message of Rattenbury, when he affirms that Word and Sacrament held together is "the most evangelical service of the Christian church" (*Thoughts on Holy Communion*, 7).

58. See Hickman, *Worshipping With United Methodists*, 24. He strongly asserts: "Today in the power of the Holy Spirit, the same living God does for congregations gathered in worship, week after week, what he did for those disciples on the first Easter Day, but with this difference: now we can come joyfully *expecting* an encounter with the risen Christ and focusing our attention on the fact of his presence. Christ bonds us anew to himself and to one another as his people, his family, his body. Christ enables his body to grow, gives to each member of the body the gifts needed in the roles to which he calls that person, and empowers the church corporately for its witness to the world" (24).

all hesitancy and to courageously make it happen. As Methodist clergy, it is a missional imperative that we take a pastoral leadership risk with our sacramental worship teaching *and* with our utilization of Constant Word and Sacrament in our worship services. We can claim to believe all kinds of things, but the ultimate proof of our belief is in our actions and in our living. We must actually practice what we say we believe, or our belief is hollow and empty, with little or no effect. For instance, if we say we believe in the power of prayer but seldom ever pray, we really do not believe in its power. The same goes for Holy Communion. Do we really believe, with Wesley, that Christ has chosen to be personally present and presently powerful through the Sacrament of Holy Communion?

This is the point where our sacramental retraining must come into play. We would do well to move our static belief about Holy Communion into a mode of active belief by practicing Holy Communion in constant and sustained fashion. In fact, following Wesley, we should practice it and receive it at every opportunity.[59] We would then be set to become a catalyst for unleashing the powerful work of God upon first, the church, and then, the world through the church.

We will even say to those who may still be sacramentally skeptical to give it an unrestrained shot for a year or two to see what happens.[60] Test it. There is no better time than *now*. With our current and ongoing demise, we really have nothing to lose and the whole world to gain. What if our entire Methodist Connexion were to take such an action to again become, as Ruth says, "singularly owned of God?"[61] It would be so simple to do. Constant Word and Sacrament praxis is the key. It is the point of entry and the

59. Wesley, "Duty of Constant Communion," 3:428–31. Note Wesley's intentional use of "constant" rather than "frequent." He states emphatically: "I say 'constantly' receiving. For as to the phrase of 'frequent communion,' it is absurd to the last degree. If it means anything less than constant it means more than can be proved to be the duty of any man. For if we are not obliged to communicate 'constantly,' by what argument can it be proved that we are obliged to communicate 'frequently'? Yea, more than once a year, or once in seven years? Or once before we die? Every argument brought for this either proves that we ought to do it *constantly*, or proves nothing at all" (431).

60. For those of us who may not yet fully believe in the efficacy of our sacramentalism, perhaps we should make a Constant Communion application of Peter Bohler's renowned advice: "Administer the Sacrament until we believe, and then because we believe, we will administer the Sacrament." Note: Bohler's original admonition was to "preach faith" and is found in Wesley, "Journal (March 4, 1738)," 1:86.

61. See Ruth, *Little Heaven Below*, 120.

apparatus for new life. We challenge Methodism to make it happen and to see through our actions what God will make happen.

Are we Methodists ready for the work of God to be unleashed? Are we ready for Methodism to be the catalyst of yet another new Pentecost?

God has decisively acted in Christ; and Christ says, "Do this." Therefore, there is only one real answer since "not ready" is not a valid response. For United Methodism to be revived, there can be no more excuses. Christ showed us his presence and power through Constant Word and Sacrament praxis during the time of the Acts 2 church. Christ then again showed us his same divine presence and power through Constant Word and Sacrament praxis during the Methodist-Evangelical Revival. We have now been given two millennia to view this work of God. We Methodists were born of this work of God. How much more being made ready to unleash it do we require?

God has indeed decisively acted in Christ, and Christ says, "Do this." His presence and his power are just as available to us now as they were to the apostles and the Wesleys. The real question is this: How will we choose in our *now* to respond?

We conclude with the refrain from an old 1912 American Methodist camp meeting hymn that proclaims, in essence, a recapitulation of Wesley's burning desire for a return to the power of the Acts 2 church. This is the very same longing that we all can and should have in our hearts for contemporary United Methodism as well:

> Lord, send the old time pow'r, The Pentecostal pow'r!
> Thy floodgates of blessing on us throw open wide!
>
> Lord, send the old-time pow'r, the Pentecostal pow'r,
> That sinners be converted and thy name glorified![62]
> (*Cokesbury* 1938, Hymn 243)

---

62. This is the refrain from the old Methodist camp meeting hymn called "Pentecostal Power" and is taken from the 1938 edition of *The Cokesbury Worship Hymnal* (#243). It was composed and published by Charles H. Gabriel (1856–1932) in 1912.

A Wesleyan-Methodist Model
For Making Disciples in the Local Church

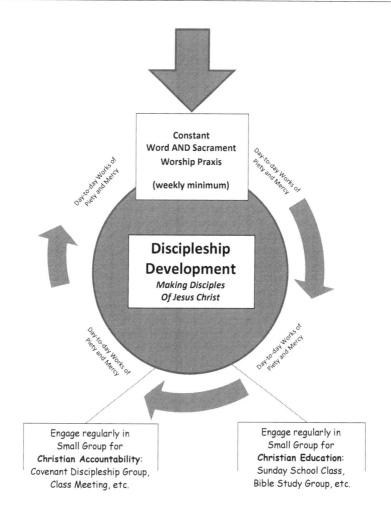

Constant
Word AND Sacrament
Worship Praxis

(weekly minimum)

Day-to-day Works of Piety and Mercy

Day-to-day Works of Piety and Mercy

Discipleship Development
Making Disciples Of Jesus Christ

Day-to-day Works of Piety and Mercy

Day-to-day Works of Piety and Mercy

Engage regularly in Small Group for **Christian Accountability**: Covenant Discipleship Group, Class Meeting, etc.

Engage regularly in Small Group for **Christian Education**: Sunday School Class, Bible Study Group, etc.

Bibliography

von Allmen, Jean-Jacques. *Worship: Its Theology and Practice*. New York: Oxford University Press, 1965.

Baker, Frank. *John Wesley and the Church of England*. London: Epworth, 1970.

Bates, Matthew W. *Salvation by Allegiance Alone*. Grand Rapids: Baker, 2017.

Billman, Frank H. *The Supernatural Thread in Methodism*. Lake Mary, FL: Creation House, 2013.

Bonhoeffer, Dietrich. *The Cost of Discipleship*. New York: Macmillan, 1961.

Borgen, Ole E. *John Wesley on the Sacraments*. Grand Rapids: Francis Asbury, 1972.

Bouyer, Louis. *The Word, Church and Sacraments*. San Francisco: Ignatius, 2004.

Bowmer, John C. *The Sacrament of the Lord's Supper in Early Methodism*. London: Dacre, 1951.

Bradshaw, Paul F. *Early Christian Worship*. Collegeville, MN: Liturgical, 2010.

Campbell, Ted A. *John Wesley and Christian Antiquity*. Nashville: Kingswood, 1991.

Cantalamessa, Raniero. *The Mystery of God's Word*. Collegeville, MN: Liturgical, 1994.

Carter, Kenneth H. *A Way of Life in the World*. Nashville: Abingdon, 2004.

Chan, Simon. *Liturgical Theology*. Downers Grove, IL: InterVarsity, 2006.

Chappell, Bryan. *Christ-Centered Worship*. Grand Rapids: Baker, 2009.

Chauvet, Louis-Marie. *The Sacraments*. Collegeville, MN: Liturgical, 2001.

Cherry, Constance M. *The Worship Architect*. Grand Rapids: Baker, 2010.

Chilcote, Paul W. *Early Methodist Spirituality*. Nashville: Kingswood, 2007.

———. "Eucharist and Formation." In *A Wesleyan Theology of the Eucharist*, edited by Jason E. Vickers, 183–201. Nashville: General Board of Higher Education and Ministry, The United Methodist Church, 2016.

———. "The Fullness of Learning." In *Cultivating a Thoughtful Faith*, edited by Maxie Dunham and Steve G. W. Moore, 63–75. Nashville: Abingdon, 2005.

———. *The Imitation of Christ*. Woodstock, VT: Skylight Paths, 2012.

———. *John & Charles Wesley: Selections from Their Writings and Hymns*. Woodstock, VT: Skylight Paths, 2011.

———. *Recapturing the Wesleys' Vision*. Downers Grove, IL: InterVarsity, 2004.

———. "The Wesleyan Tradition." In *The Wesleyan Tradition*, edited by Paul W. Chilcote, 23–37. Nashville: Abingdon, 2002.

Chung-Kim, Esther. "The Lord's Supper: Banquet for All." Christ Church, Oxford University, Oxford, UK: Wesley Studies and Early Methodist Working Group. Twelfth Oxford Institute of Methodist Theological Studies, 2007.

Coleman, Robert E. *Nothing to Do but to Save Souls*. Nappanee, IN: Evangel, 1990.

Collins, Gary R. *Beyond Easy Believism*. Waco, TX: Word, 1982.

Collins, Jim. *Good to Great*. New York: HarperCollins, 2001.

Collins, Kenneth J. *The Scripture Way of Salvation*. Nashville: Abingdon, 1997.

———. *The Theology of John Wesley: Holy Love and the Shape of Grace*. Nashville: Abingdon, 2007.

Conzelmann, Hans. *History of Primitive Christianity*. Nashville: Abingdon, 1973.

Cordeiro, Wayne. *Jesus: Pure & Simple*. Minneapolis: Bethany House, 2012.

Craddock, Fred B. "Hebrews." In *The New Interpreter's Bible*, Vol. 12, edited by Leander E. Keck, 3–173. 13 vols. Nashville: Abingdon, 1998.

Crowe, John Marshall. *Church Health for the Twenty-First Century*. Little Elm, TX: eLectio, 2017.

Culpepper, R. Alan. "Luke." In *The New Interpreter's Bible*, Vol. 10, edited by Leander E. Keck, . 13 vols. Nashville: Abingdon, 1995.

Davies, William R. *Spirit Baptism and Spiritual Gifts*. Warrington, UK: W. R. Davies, 1973.

Davis, John Jefferson. *Worship and the Reality of God*. Downers Grove, IL: IVP, 2010.

Dayton, Donald W. *Theological Roots of Pentecostalism*. Grand Rapids: Baker, 1987.

DeSilva, David A. *Sacramental Life*. Downers Grove, IL: IVP, 2008.

Dix, Dom Gregory. *The Shape of the Liturgy*. London: Bloomsbury, 2015.

Dunn, James D. G. "2 Timothy." In *The New Interpreter's Bible*, Vol. 11, edited by Leander E. Keck, 832–60. 13 vols. Nashville: Abingdon, 2000.

Earle, Ralph. "1 Timothy." In *The Expositor's Bible Commentary*, Vol. 11, edited by Frank E. Gabelein, 339–90. 12 vols. Grand Rapids: Zondervan, 1978.

Etheridge, John Wesley. *The Life of the Rev. Adam Clarke*. New York: Carlton & Porter, 1859.

Felton, Gayle Carlton. *By Water and the Spirit*. Nashville: Discipleship Resources, 1997.

———. *This Gift of Water*. Nashville: Abingdon, 1992.

———. *This Holy Mystery*. Nashville: Discipleship Resources, 2007.

———. *United Methodists and the Sacraments*. Nashville: Abingdon, 2007.

Gealy, Fred D. "1 Timothy." In *The Interpreter's Bible*, Vol. 11, edited by George Arthur Buttrick, 375–459. 12 vols. Nashville: Abingdon, 1955.

Hahn, Scott. *Consuming the Word*. New York: Image, 2013.

———. *The Lamb's Supper*. New York: Doubleday, 1999.

Hamilton, Adam. *Revival: Faith as Wesley Lived it*. Nashville: Abingdon, 2014.

Harper, Steve. *Devotional Life in the Wesleyan Tradition*. Nashville: The Upper Room, 1983.

———. *Five Marks of a Methodist*. Nashville: Abingdon, 2015.

———. *Prayer & Devotional Life of United Methodists*. Nashville: Abingdon, 1999.

———. *The Way to Heaven*. Grand Rapids: Zondervan, 2003.

Heath, Elaine A. "Reading Scripture for Christian Formation." In *Wesley, Wesleyans, and Reading Bible as Scripture*, edited by Joel B. Green and David F. Watson, 211–25. Waco, TX: Baylor University Press, 2012.

Hickman, Hoyt L. *Worshipping With United Methodists*. Nashville: Abingdon, 1996.

Hicks, John Mark. *Come to the Table*. Abilene, TX: Leafwood, 2002.

Hildebrandt, Franz. *Christianity According to the Wesleys*. Grand Rapids: Baker, 1996.

Horton, Michael. *A Better Way*. Grand Rapids: Baker, 2002.

Hyatt, Eddie L. *2000 Years of Charismatic Christianity*. Lake Mary, FL: Charisma House, 2002.

Ignatius, Saint. "The Epistle of Ignatius to the Ephesians." In *Ante-Nicene Fathers*, Vol. 1, edited by Alexander Roberts and James Donaldson, 49–58. 10 vols. Peabody, MA: Hendrickson, 2012.

Ingram, Chip. *Good to Great in God's Eyes*. Grand Rapids: Baker, 2007.

Irenaeus. "Against Heresies." In *Ante-Nicene Fathers*, Vol. 1, edited by Alexander Roberts and James Donaldson, 315–567. 10 vols. Peabody, MA: Hendrickson, 2012.

Jackman, John, dir. *Wesley: A Heart Transformed Can Change the World*. 2009; Worcester, PA: Foundery Pictures. DVD.

Jennings, Daniel R. *The Supernatural Occurrences of John Wesley*. S.l.: Sean Multimedia, 2012.

Jeremias, Joachim. *The Eucharistic Words of Jesus*. Philadelphia: Trinity Press International, 1990.

Jesson, Nicholas A. "*Lex orandi, lex credendi*: Towards a Liturgical Theology." Academic paper. Toronto, CAN: Toronto School of Theology (November 2001). https://www.ecumenism.net/archive/jesson_lexorandi.pdf.

Job, Rueben P. *Three Simple Rules*. Nashville: Abingdon, 2007.

———. *A Wesleyan Spiritual Reader*. Nashville: Abingdon, 1997.

Jones, Scott, and Bruce R. Ough. *Seven Vision Pathways*. Nashville: Abingdon, 2010.

Joujon, Maurice. "Justin." In *The Eucharist of the Christians*, edited by Raymond Johanny, 71–77. Collegeville, MN: Liturgical, 1990.

Justin. "The First Apology of Justin." In *Ante-Nicene Fathers*, Vol. 1, edited by Alexander Roberts and James Donaldson, 163–87. 10 vols. Peabody, MA: Hendrickson, 2012.

Keck, Leander E. *Taking the Bible Seriously*. Nashville: Abingdon, 1979.

Keefer, Luke L., Jr. "John Wesley: Disciple of Early Christianity." *Wesleyan Theological Journal* 19.1 (Spring 1984) 23–32.

à Kempis, Thomas. *The Imitation of Christ*. Chicago: Moody, 1980.

Khoo, Lorna. *Wesleyan Eucharistic Spirituality*. Hindmarsh, SA: Australian Theological Forum, 2005.

Kimbrough, S. T., Jr. *The Lyrical Theology of Charles Wesley*. Eugene, OR: Cascade, 2011.

King, Peter. *An Enquiry into the Constitution, Discipline, Unity, & Worship of the Primitive Church*. London: Seely, Burnside, and Seely, 1843.

Kinghorn, Kenneth Cain. *The Gospel of Grace*. Nashville: Abingdon, 1992.

Kinnaman, David, and Gabe Lyons. *Unchristian*. Grand Rapids: Baker, 2007.

Kisker, Scott. *Mainline or Methodist?* Nashville: Discipleship Resources, 2008.

Knight, Henry H., III. *Anticipating Heaven Below*. Eugene, OR: Cascade, 2014.

———. *Eight Life-Enriching Practices of United Methodists*. Nashville: Abingdon, 2001.

———. *The Presence of God in the Christian Life*. Lanham, MD: Scarecrow, 1987.

Kodell, Jerome. *The Eucharist in the New Testament*. Collegeville, MN: Liturgical, 1991.

Kreider, Eleanor. *Communion Shapes Character*. Scottdale, PA: Herald, 1997.

Langford, Thomas A. "Teaching in the Methodist Tradition: A Wesleyan Perspective." In *By What Authority*, edited by Elizabeth Box Price and Charles R. Foster, 57–71. Nashville: Abingdon, 1991.

Laurance, John D. *The Sacrament of the Eucharist*. Collegeville, MN: Liturgical, 2012.

LaVerdiere, Eugene. *The Breaking of the Bread*. Chicago: Liturgy Training, 1998.

———. *Dining in the Kingdom*. Chicago: Liturgy Training. 1994.

———. *The Eucharist in the New Testament and the Early Church*. Collegeville, MN: Liturgical, 1996.

Macquarrie, John. *A Guide to the Sacraments*. London: SCM, 2005.

Maddox, Randy. *Responsible Grace.* Nashville: Abingdon, 1994.

Maddox, Randy, ed. "Charles and John Wesley's 'Hymns on the Lord's Supper' (1745)." Durham, NC: Duke Center for Studies in the Wesleyan Tradition, 2009. https://divinity.duke.edu/sites/divinity.duke.edu/files/documents/cswt/27_Hymns_on_the_Lord%27s_Supper_%281745%29_mod.pdf.

Mare, W. Harold. "1 Corinthians." In *The Expositor's Bible Commentary*, Vol. 10, edited by Frank E. Gaebelein, 175–297. 12 vols. Grand Rapids: Zondervan, 1976.

Marshall, I. Howard. *Last Supper & Lord's Supper.* Vancouver: Regent College Publishing, 2006.

Martin, Ralph P. *The Worship of God.* Grand Rapids: Eerdmans, 1991.

Matthaei, Sondra Higgins. *Making Disciples.* Nashville: Abingdon, 2000.

McManus, Erwin Raphael. *An Unstoppable Force.* Loveland, CO: Group, 2001.

Mitman, F. Russell. *Worship in the Shape of Scripture.* Cleveland: Pilgrim, 2001.

Morrill, Bruce T. *Encountering Christ in the Eucharist.* New York: Paulist, 2012.

Mounce, William D. *Mounce's Complete Expository Dictionary of Old & New Testament Words.* Grand Rapids: Zondervan, 2006.

NCCUMC. Journal Archives. http://journal.nccumc.org/journals.html.

NCCUMC. "North Carolina Conference Lay/Clergy Equalization Plan for Annual Conference 2015." http://www.nccumc.org/secretary/files/LAY_EQUAL_PLAN8.pdf.

Nikodemos the Hagiorite. *Concerning Frequent Communion of the Immaculate Mysteries of Christ.* Translated by George Dokos. Thessalonika, Greece: Uncut Mountain, 2006.

Norwood. Frederick A. *Sourcebook of American Methodism.* Nashville: Abingdon, 1984.

———. *The Story of American Methodism.* Nashville: Abingdon, 1974.

Noyes, Morgan P. "1 Timothy." In *The Interpreter's Bible*, Vol. 11, edited by George Arthur Buttrick, 375–459. 12 vols. Nashville: Abingdon, 1955.

O'Day, Gail R. "John." In *The New Interpreter's Bible*, Vol. 9, edited by Leander E. Keck, 491–865. 13 vols. Nashville: Abingdon, 1995.

Oden, Thomas C. *Classical Pastoral Care.* Grand Rapids: Baker, 1987.

———. *Classic Christianity.* New York: HarperCollins, 1992.

———. *John Wesley's Scriptural Christianity.* Grand Rapids: Zondervan, 1994.

———. *John Wesley's Teachings.* 4 Vols. Grand Rapids: Zondervan, 2012 (Vols. 1–3), 2014 (Vol. 4).

Oh, Gwang Seok. *John Wesley's Ecclesiology.* Lanham, MD: Scarecrow, 2008.

Outler, Albert C. *John Wesley.* New York: Oxford University Press, 1980.

Payne, William P. *American Methodism: Past & Future Growth.* Lexington, KY: Emeth, 2013.

Pfatteicher, Philip H. *Liturgical Spirituality.* Harrisburg, PA: Trinity Press International, 1997.

Rainer, Thom S., and Eric Geiger. *Simple Church.* Nashville: B&H, 2006.

Rattenbury, J. Ernest. *The Eucharistic Hymns of John and Charles Wesley.* 1948. Reprint. Akron, OH: OSL, 2006.

———. *Thoughts on Holy Communion.* 1958. Reprint. Eugene, OR: Wipf & Stock, 2016.

———. *Wesley's Legacy to the World.* Reprint. 1938. Eugene, OR: Wipf & Stock, 2009.

Ross, Allen P. *Recalling the Hope of Glory.* Grand Rapids: Kregel, 2006.

Ruth, Lester. *Early Methodist Life and Spirituality.* Nashville: Kingswood, 2005.

———. *A Little Heaven Below.* Nashville: Kingswood, 2000.

———. "Word and Table: A Wesleyan Model for Balanced Worship." In *Wesleyan Tradition*, edited by Paul W. Chilcote, 136–47. Nashville: Abingdon, 2002.

Sampley, J. Paul. "I Corinthians." In *The New Interpreter's Bible*, Vol. 10, edited by Leander E. Keck, 771–1003. 12 vols. Nashville: Abingdon, 2002.

Schaff, Philip. *The Didache*. Buckshaw Village, UK: Christian Books Today, 2013.

Schaller, Lyle E. *The Ice Cube is Melting*. Nashville: Abingdon, 2004.

Schaper, Robert. *In His Presence: Appreciating Your Worship Tradition*. Nashville: Thomas Nelson, 1984.

Schillebeeckx, Edward. *Christ the Sacrament of the Encounter with God*. London: Rowman & Littlefield, 1987.

Schmemann, Alexander. *The Eucharist*. Crestwood, NY: St. Vladimir's Seminary Press, 1987.

———. *For the Life of the World*. Crestwood, NY: St. Vladimir's Seminary Press, 1973.

Schnase, Robert. *Five Practices of Fruitful Congregations*. Nashville: Abingdon, 2007.

Senn, Frank C. *A Stewardship of the Mysteries*. Mahwah, NJ: Paulist, 1999.

Smith, Gordon T. *Evangelical, Sacramental & Pentecostal*. Downers Grove, IL: IVP, 2017.

Smith, James K. A. *Desiring the Kingdom*. Grand Rapids: Baker, 2009.

Snyder, Howard A. *The Divided Flame*. Eugene, OR: Wipf & Stock, 2011.

———. *The Radical Wesley and Patterns for Church Renewal*. Eugene, OR: Wipf & Stock, 1996.

Spinks, Bryan D. "Anglicans and Dissenters." In *The Oxford History of Christian Worship*, edited by Geoffrey Wainwright and Karen B. Westerfield-Tucker, 492–533. New York: Oxford University Press, 2006.

Stallings, W. Joseph. *The Genesis Column*. Eugene, OR: Wipf & Stock, 2018.

———. *The Necessity of Constant Word and Sacrament Praxis for the Propagation of Christian Discipleship Within United Methodism*. Ashland, OH: Ashland Theological Seminary, 2016.

Staples, Rob L. *Outward Sign and Inward Grace*. Kansas City: Beacon Hill, 1991.

Stetzer, Ed, and Thom S. Rainer. *Transformational Church*. Nashville: B&H, 2010.

Stillingfleet, Edward. *Irenicum: A Weapon Salve for the Church's Wounds*. Philadelphia: M. Sorin, 1842.

Stokes, Mack B. *The Bible in the Wesleyan Heritage*. Nashville: Abingdon, 1981.

Stookey, Lawrence Hull. *Eucharist: Christ's Feast With the Church*. Nashville: Abingdon, 1993.

Thompson, Bard. *Liturgies of the Western Church*. Cleveland: William Collins, 1962.

Tyson, John R. *The Way of the Wesleys*. Grand Rapids: Eerdmans, 2014.

UMC-NCC. journal.nccumc.org/tables2015.html.

The United Methodist Book of Discipline (BOD). Nashville: United Methodist, 2016.

The United Methodist Book of Worship (UMBOW). Nashville: United Methodist, 1992.

The United Methodist Hymnal (UMH). Nashville: United Methodist, 1989.

Vahanian, Gabriel. *The Death of God*. New York: George Braziller, 2011.

———. *Wait Without Idols*. Eugene, OR: Wipf & Stock, 2010.

Wainwright, Geoffrey. *Eucharist and Eschatology*. Akron, OH: OSL, 2002.

Walker, Williston, et al. *A History of the Christian Church*. New York: Charles Scribner's Sons, 1985.

Wall, Clifford W. "The End of Salvation: *The Image of God* in John Wesley's Soteriology with Insight from Thomas Aquinas." Academic paper. Dayton, OH: United Theological Seminary, 2018.

Wall, Robert W. "Acts." In *The New Interpreter's Bible*, Vol. 10, edited by Leander E. Keck, 2–368. 13 vols. Nashville: Abingdon, 2002.

———. "Wesley as Biblical Interpreter." In *The Cambridge Companion to John Wesley*, edited by Randy L. Maddox and Jason E. Vickers, 113–28. New York: Cambridge University Press, 2010.

Warren, Rick. *The Purpose Driven Church*. Grand Rapids: Zondervan, 1995.

Watson, David Lowes. *The Early Methodist Class Meeting*. 1985. Reprint. Eugene, OR: Wipf & Stock, 2002.

Watson, Kevin M. *A Blueprint for Discipleship*. Nashville: Discipleship Resources, 2009.

Webber, Robert E. *Ancient-Future Worship*. Grand Rapids: Baker, 2008.

———. *Liturgical Evangelism*. Harrisburg, PA: Morehouse, 1986.

———. *Who Gets to Narrate the World?* Downers Grove, IL: InterVarsity, 2008.

———. *Worship is a Verb*. Peabody, MA: Hendrickson, 1999.

———. *Worship Old & New*. Grand Rapids: Zondervan, 1994.

Weems, Lovett H., and Tom Berlin. *Overflow*. Nashville: Abingdon, 2013.

Wesley, Charles. "Journal (April 14, 1745)." In *The Journal of Charles Wesley*, Vol. 1, edited by Thomas Jackson, 396. 2 vols. Grand Rapids, MI: Baker, 1980.

Wesley, John. "Causes of the Inefficacy of Christianity." In *The Works of John Wesley*, Vol. 4, edited by Albert C. Outler, 85–96. 35 vols. . Nashville: Abingdon, 1987.

———. "The Duty of Constant Communion." In *The Works of John Wesley*, Vol. 3, edited by Albert C. Outler, 427–39. 35 vols. Nashville: Abingdon, 1986.

———. "An Earnest Appeal to Men of Reason and Religion." In *The Works of Wesley*, Vol. 11, edited by Gerald R. Cragg, 37–94. 35 vols. Nashville: Abingdon.

———. *Explanatory Notes upon the New Testament*. London: Forgotten, 2012.

———. "A Farther Appeal to Men of Reason and Religion." In *The Works of John Wesley*, Vol. 8, edited by Thomas Jackson, 46–247. 14 vols. Grand Rapids: Baker, 1996.

———. "The General Deliverance." In *The Works of John Wesley*, Vol. 2, edited by Albert C. Outler, 436–50. 35 vols. Nashville: Abingdon, 1985.

———. "General Rules of the United Societies." In *The Works of John Wesley*, Vol. 9, edited by Ruppert E. Davies, 67–79. 35 vols. Nashville: Abingdon, 1989.

———. "God's Approbation of His Works." In *The Works of John Wesley*, Vol. 2, edited by Albert C. Outler, 387–99. 35 vols. Nashville: Abingdon, 1985.

———. "Heavenly Treasure in Earthen Vessels." In *The Works of John Wesley*, Vol. 4, edited by Albert C. Outler, 161–67. 35 vols. Nashville: Abingdon, 1987.

———. "Journal (January 20, 1746)." In *The Works of John Wesley*, Vol. 2, edited by Thomas Jackson, 6–7. 14 vols. Grand Rapids: Baker, 1996.

———. "Journal (June 2, 1766)." In *The Works of John Wesley*, Vol. 3, edited by Thomas Jackson, 251. 14 vols. Grand Rapids: Baker, 1996.

———. "Journal (October 28, 1762)." In *The Works of John Wesley*, Vol. 21, edited by W. Reginald Ward and Richard P. Heitzenrater, 392. 35 vols. Nashville: Abingdon, 1992.

———. "Journal (September 1, 1784)." In *The Works of John Wesley*, Vol. 4, edited by Thomas Jackson, 288. 14 vols. Grand Rapids: Baker, 1996.

———. "Large Minutes 1753–1763." In *The Works of John Wesley*, Vol. 10, edited by Henry D. Rack, 845–74. 35 vols. Nashville: Abingdon, 2011.

———. "Letter to Dr. Coke, Mr. Asbury, and Our Brethren in America (September 10, 1784)." In *The Works of John Wesley*, Vol. 13, edited by Thomas Jackson, 251–52. 14 vols. Grand Rapids: Baker, 1996.

———. "Letter to his Brother Charles (June 8, 1780)." In *The Works of John Wesley*, Vol. 12, edited by Thomas Jackson, 147–48. 14 vols. Grand Rapids: Baker, 1996.

———. "Letters to a Member of the Society. Letter CCLVIII (April 14, 1771)." In *The Works of John Wesley*, Vol. 12, edited by Thomas Jackson, 289–90. 14 vols. Grand Rapids: Baker, 1996.

———. "The Marks of the New Birth." In *The Works of John Wesley*, Vol. 1, edited by Albert C. Outler, 417–30. 35 vols. Nashville: Abingdon, 1984.

———. "The Means of Grace." In *The Works of John Wesley*, Vol. 1, edited by Albert C. Outler, 376–97. 35 vols. Nashville: Abingdon, 1984.

———. "Minutes of Several Conversations." In *The Works of John Wesley*, Vol. 8, edited by Thomas Jackson, 299. 14 vols. Grand Rapids: Baker, 1996.

———. "The New Birth." In *The Works of John Wesley*, Vol. 2, edited by Albert C. Outler, 186–201. 35 vols. Nashville: Abingdon, 1985.

———. "On a Single Eye." In *The Works of John Wesley*, Vol. 4, edited by Albert C. Outler, 120–30. 35 vols. Nashville: Abingdon, 1987.

———. "On Laying the Foundation of the New Chapel." In *The Works of John Wesley*, Vol. 3, edited by Albert C. Outler, 579–92. 35 vols. Nashville: Abingdon, 1986.

———. "On the Church." In *The Works of John Wesley*, Vol. 13, edited by Thomas Jackson, 253–54. 14 vols. Grand Rapids: Baker, 1996.

———. "On Working Out Our Own Salvation." In *The Works of John Wesley*, Vol. 3, edited by Albert C. Outler, 199–209. 35 vols. Nashville: Abingdon, 1986.

———. *A Plain Account of Christian Perfection.* Transcribed by Kenneth Cain Kinghorn. Lexington, KY: Emeth, 2012.

———. "Preface to Standard Sermons." In *The Works of John Wesley*, Vol. 1, edited by Albert C. Outler, 103–7. 35 vols. Nashville: Abingdon, 1984.

———. "The Scripture Way of Salvation." In *The Works of John Wesley*, Vol. 2, edited by Albert C. Outler, 153–69. 35 vols. Nashville: Abingdon, 1986.

———. "Thoughts upon Methodism." In *The Works of John Wesley*, Vol. 9, edited by Rupert E. Davies, 527–30. 35 vols. Nashville: Abingdon, 1989.

———. "A Treatise on Baptism." In *The Works of John Wesley*, Vol. 10, edited by Thomas Jackson, 188–201. 14 vols. Grand Rapids: Baker, 1996.

———. "Upon Our Lord's Sermon on the Mount – Discourse VI." In *The Works of John Wesley*, Vol. 1, edited by Albert C. Outler, 572–91. 35 vols. Nashville: Abingdon, 1984.

———. "The Witness of Our Own Spirit." In *The Works of John Wesley*, Vol. 1, edited by Albert C. Outler, 299–313. 35 vols. Nashville: Abingdon, 1984.

———. "The Witness of the Spirit, I." In *The Works of John Wesley*, Vol. 1, edited by Albert C. Outler, 267–84. 35 vols. Nashville: Abingdon, 1984.

Westerfield-Tucker, Karen B. *American Methodist Worship.* New York: Oxford University Press, 2001.

White, James F. *A Brief History of Christian Worship.* Nashville: Abingdon, 1993.

———. *Sacraments as God's Self Giving.* Nashville: Abingdon, 1983.

———. *The Sacraments in Protestant Practice and Faith.* Nashville: Abingdon, 1999.

Wilke, Richard B. *And are We Yet Alive?* Nashville: Abingdon, 1986.

Williams, Rowan. *Being Christian.* Grand Rapids: Eerdmans, 2014.

———. *Being Disciples.* Grand Rapids: Eerdmans, 2016.

Willimon, William H. *The Service of God.* Nashville: Abingdon, 1983.

Willimon, William H., and Robert L. Wilson. *Rekindling the Flame.* Nashville: Abingdon, 1987.

Witherington, Ben, III. *Making a Meal of it.* Waco, TX: Baylor University Press, 2007.

Wood, A. Skevington. *The Burning Heart.* Lexington, KY: Emeth, 2007.

Wood, Laurence W. *The Meaning of Pentecost in Early Methodism.* Lanham, MD: Scarecrow, 2002.

Yrigoyen, Charles, Jr. *John Wesley: Holiness of Heart and Life.* New York: General Board of Global Ministries, The United Methodist Church, 1996.

———. *Praising the God of Grace.* Nashville: Abingdon, 2005.